"Insightful, challenging and refresh
your thinking and change your definition of traditional employment. The thought that you are "employed by God" changes the way you work and live your life."

Mark Quattrochi
Pastor (Grace Family Church-Eastlake)

"*Employed for Life* has taken my insight about God's plan for employment to deeper levels than any other book I have read. Working for God and never being unemployed is one of the many employment strategies that radically changes your perspective on how you conduct your job search. If you are looking for true purpose and vision at whatever state of employment you are in, *Employed for Life* is the book you must read."

Tim Krauss MS
Job Connection

"Dear Barb, . . . Your book . . . has played a very important part in growing an area of my relationship with Jesus that really needed to be challenged—Trust/Faith. God has really used you as a vehicle to minister to so many, and I believe He will continue to do so as you have a gift for this. I will share your book with all those that will benefit, which is pretty much everyone!"

Nicole Spencer
Reader

"If you are unemployed and looking for a job, then get a copy of *Employed for Life* right now. Its pages have answers to your prayers, even those you have not yet prayed. A great combination of truth about you, your situation, job seeker tips and the God who loves you."

Brian Ray
Founder and President,
Crossroads Career Network

EMPLOYED for LIFE

"When Can You Start?"
- God

BARBARA
RARDEN

Employed for Life: "When Can You Start?" – God

ISBN: 978-1-56427-297-3
Category: Religious / Christian Living / Self-Help

Published in cooperation with Crown Financial Ministries, Inc. This revised edition is based on *The Gospel of Unemployment* by Barbara Rarden.

Cover Design: Sean Allen

Printed in the United States of America.

CONTENTS

DEDICATION

In gratitude to God for the wise counsel and enduring friendship of my father, Victor Palmer, and the steadfast support and continual love of my mother, Marian.

PREFACE

I believe that you and I are meeting here, on these pages, by divine appointment. I encourage you to open your heart and mind to the message presented here and allow God to show you a radically different way to look at job changes and your career.

I've been working with small groups of Christian job seekers for more than 20 years now. I cannot count the miracles I've seen and the amazing journeys I've witnessed. Now I want to share those stories with you and share the secrets God has revealed on this very topic. You may not see any scriptures here that aren't already familiar but you might discover a new way to view, understand and apply what we've been given in God's Word.

What you read here may well cause you to reconsider your interpretation of God's Word as we go through this journey together. Many of the verses I will be using are popular in the "prosperity gospel" circuit. For this reason I would like to stop right here and clearly distance myself and this message from that twisted "theology." My goal in writing this book is to *bring people into a right relationship with God the Father, Jesus His Son, and the Holy Spirit.*

I have witnessed the difference it has made in countless lives when people (including believers) understand that God is seeking to be in personal relationship with us, that He will never leave us or forsake us in this life, and that He desires to bring us into eternal life to be with Him forever! That IS the good news, "gospel," that I will be writing about. I will neither make promises, nor hopefully imply, that we can use God's Word to bend Him to our will, that we can command material things to come into our lives at our beckoning through the exercising of our faith, or that this life is meant to be equal to Heaven in the pleasure and joy we will experience there.

As you come through these pages with me, I hope you will experience the fullness of the five blessings God is offering to job seekers and working believers. There is no doubt that you will find them more than enough to satisfy. In my years working with job seekers, I have seen that God is good and is love, to a measure that far exceeds our limited understanding of those words. Now with this book I hope to invite you to come very near to Jesus, the Good Shepherd, so that during times of employment changes you will find peace and eternal safety with Him and receive all you will ever need in His hand.

I'll share what I've learned so that you can see where I began to discover God's view of unemployment. You'll see that I started by finding out about the forces job seekers were up against and then learned, over time, how God wanted to deal with the situation with and through His children in the workplace.

I'll also tell you how the book ends right now, so you won't wonder. We win! We win satisfying and challenging work assignments and much, much more. We also gain strong faith in the name of Jesus, peace, guidance, confidence and all that comes with a deep, personal relationship with God.

If you weren't aware of it, you'll discover that there is a spiritual battle going on and we are wrestling against powers and principalities in addition to human error and foolishness as we go through our employment experiences. But we don't wrestle alone. The Spirit of the living God is with us in this battle and now is the time to learn how to win the war for the workplace. Far more importantly, God has His own agenda in response to job loss and career transitions. You see, He never views you as unemployed. As far as He's concerned, you are one of His royal children, working on assignment for Him. So the biggest part of this book is devoted to that perspective. We're going to explore what God has in mind for His children while they're both in and out of the workplace. That's where you'll find even more good news!

You see, God is very interested in the workplace, and He is ready to lead believers in triumph as they make job changes. Perhaps you've already noticed that the very best job search tactics and techniques the world has to offer are failing. The idea that a job seeker would be better off just concentrating on getting good at those methods at the expense of seeking God's way and wisdom is not only foolish, it's impractical. When you recall that Jesus was able to take a measly amount of food in a little boy's hand and feed thousands without the use of carryout, you have to acknowledge that no technique taught in a job search seminar can match that kind of performance. The good news is that God's arm is still strong to care for those who choose to follow after Him.

Finally, if you're not sure about all this "spiritual talk" and how it could possibly relate to *your* life and situation, don't worry. Keep an open mind and heart and stay with me. I guarantee it'll all begin to make sense as we go along. Oh, and if you're worried that you might not be "spiritual" enough to be up to the task, you can let that worry go too. This message is for brand new believers, mature believers and even those who just want to check out the whole Jesus thing.

CHAPTER 1

INTRODUCTION

"Yes, I am the gate. Those who come in through me will be saved. They will come and go freely and will find good pastures."

– John 10:9

My guess is that you've decided to read this book because you're eager—even desperate—for help finding a job or changing careers. Relax and take a deep breath. I can assure you, what follows will be the most powerful and effective employment strategy you could ever hope to find. I know this, because it's nothing less than God's plan for you.

First, however, you must understand the true nature of unemployment and work. This is critical before you can move forward. Believe it or not, unemployment is neither bad nor good. It is actually a neutral life event. You can experience it either way, good or bad. It's up to you.

Think about it. There are many people who daily look forward to unemployment. It's something they wait for their entire work lives. Of course, that form of unemployment is called "retirement," but it is nonetheless unemployment.

Sabbaticals are another form of unemployment enjoyed in some professions. Imagine being paid not to work! Some of us have had the wonderful experience of temporarily leaving the workplace to have a baby, raise children or pursue some life goal such as travel or study. All of these seasons of unemployment are perceived as good, right?

Then again, there are times when unemployment is thrust upon you, when you aren't ready to lose a job or a business. When that happens, the loss of income, relationships with co-workers, and the opportunity to be productive can be depressing. But if you could somehow separate the actual experience of unemployment from the anticipation of financial hardship and emotional pain, you might see it as something else entirely. After all, how often do you get a break from the day-to-day grind to pursue things your heart really desires? But I'm getting ahead of myself. For now, just try to accept the idea that unemployment is a neutral experience with potential for either a good or bad outcome.

Consider a team of archaeologists who have determined that a treasure the size of King Solomon's lies buried in a remote part of Africa. They've spent months securing funding and gathering supplies to find the treasure. You can practically feel their excitement as the plane finally touches down on a dusty airstrip in Africa and their adventure begins. Now imagine another plane just like it but filled with business travelers headed for Europe. Due to mechanical difficultics, this plane is forced to make an emergency landing at the same isolated airstrip as the archaeologists. It's not difficult to imagine this group's fear and apprehension as they step off the plane.

Here you have two groups of travelers, in exactly the same place, facing the same conditions, yet their reactions couldn't differ more. Conclusion: Being stranded on a desolate airstrip in the middle of nowhere can be good or bad, depending on who's stranded.

Obviously, the archaeologists were prepared for the journey and had provisions and resources to sustain themselves. They also had a specific goal in mind and the promise of great return if they achieved it. The unfortunate business travelers, on the other hand, were waylaid from their intended destination and put in a precarious situation with no resources.

Preparation dramatically affected how the two groups viewed their surroundings. Because they were ready for the experience, the scientists had their eyes wide open to take in the wonder of their surroundings and were on the lookout for the riches they expected to find. Meanwhile, the distressed business travelers weren't interested in sightseeing or adventure. They just wanted out! Now, if somehow, miraculously, they had food, shelter and arrangements for rescue, chances are good this otherwise frightening experience would quickly become a great story to tell the folks back home.

Here's the bottom line: You can't experience a positive and productive time of joblessness unless you're open to the possibility that unemployment is not a guaranteed tragedy! I'll assume you're with me on this even though you might be unemployed right now and thinking, "I don't have sustaining resources. I didn't choose to be here, and this is messing up my life in a very uncomfortable way."

You probably see yourself in the business travelers' situation, not that of the team of archaeologists. That's all right. We'll get to the matter of resources soon enough, but please stay open to the idea that if you're out of a job, your current circumstance has the potential to be a good one filled with adventure and possibilities.

If you're currently employed but wondering what your work future holds, you have the opportunity right now to prepare like the archaeologists and get ready for your next career journey. And that preparation can start with another important truth: Unemployment is not a guaranteed financial disaster.

Unemployment is not a guaranteed financial disaster.

I've been involved in ministries supporting job seekers for more than two decades and I've seen two very significant things related to financial well-being in that time. First, God has always spoken to His people about the importance of stewardship in order to prepare them for their life experiences. By understanding and practicing the principles of His economy, believers can prepare for job changes and transitions and be spared much of the trauma that others experience with job loss. And second, thanks to the grace and mercy of God, I have seen how even those who have not been taught these principles, or who have not employed them, have experienced the wonderful intervention of God in their time of need. I've personally received financial blessings in times of unemployment, and I've seen them poured out on others when no earthly source was available to meet the need.

To illustrate, one night I was leading a small group session for job seekers when a young woman joined us. She was very upset and began to tell her story. That morning she had been let go from her job without warning. She was single and living on her own with no savings and no family or friends to rely on for help. We prayed together, and I shared some biblical principles that apply to job seekers. She was open to the truths that we discussed and left the meeting still nervous but hopeful.

The next week she was back with a smile on her face. To her surprise, she did have family to help her. She had received an inheritance check from the estate of a relative she never knew and the amount met her immediate financial needs.

We spent that meeting praising God and exploring what she really wanted to do in her next work assignment. She was fluent in multiple languages and believed that God had given her this gift as a way to bless others, so she wanted to be a translator for the United Nations.

She hadn't been able to act on that dream until a season of unemployment and an unexpected financial blessing provided the time and resources to pursue it. So, again we prayed and again we looked to God to meet her needs and to guide her. That night we all left with greater faith and hope.

The next week this young woman was back with an even bigger grin! This time she told us that her former company had offered a settlement pertaining to her layoff. With that extra sum and the inheritance she had far more money unemployed than while she was working!

The final chapter of her story came a few weeks later. She showed up with a letter from a local university looking for people interested in foreign language translation as a career. The school was offering free tuition, books and a stipend. Needless to say, that's where she was headed the last time we saw her.

God will give you exactly what you need to be transformed from a frightened traveler to an excited adventurer.

Don't leap to the conclusion that this will happen for you if you "do it right." Nothing I will tell you in this book is to be construed as a "formula for success" as the world defines it. You need to lift your eyes far above these earthly circumstances and considerations to see what God is offering to help you—Himself! The point is, God will give you exactly what you need to be transformed from a frightened traveler to an excited adventurer. Just allow that possibility to open your mind and heart as we look at one other foundational truth about unemployment.

Unemployment is not a personal phenomenon. Asking, "Why me?" is simply not useful. A better question is, "Why is there unemployment?" and Matthew 5:45 holds the answer:

> *"For he gives his sunlight to both the evil and the good, and he sends rain on the just and the unjust alike."*

That goes for unemployment, too. It can impact anyone at any time. These days, the average time in a single job is not quite 4.5 years in the U.S. This means workers will change jobs 7 to 10 times in the course of their careers. Since baby boomers are influencing this statistic with longer periods of tenure, younger workers are likely to experience 14 or more job changes. It's unlikely that all of them will be voluntary.[1] Think about your family and friends. How many of them have been out of work? One? Five? Many of us could name 10 or more people who've lost jobs in recent years. That's why this is a message for every believer, whether currently employed or not.

The question is how do we prepare for this likely future event? Well, in the Bible we see how two identical houses fared very differently when storms came against them. Only one withstood the assault without falling, and that was the one built on a rock.[2] So

---

1. Bureau of Labor Statistics, http://www.bls.gov/news.release/pdf/tenure.pdf.
2. Matthew 7:24-25

our goal, first and foremost, is to make sure we, like the wise man, are building on a secure foundation. *"He is the Rock, His work is perfect; For all His ways are justice, a God of truth and without injustice; Righteous and upright is He"* (Deuteronomy 32:4, NKJV). With Jesus as the chief cornerstone in our lives we, too, will successfully weather the storms of life.

Don't misunderstand; I'm not saying God is behind this workplace turbulence or that He causes us to be unemployed. I am saying that this is an experience common to man, and that God has a solution for us. *"And we know that all things work together for good to those who love God, to those who are called according to His purpose"* (Romans 8:28 NKJV).

It's important to realize that situations are not the determining factors in our lives; what really matters is our preparation for, and our response to, those situations. And be assured that unemployment is not reserved for those who have done something wrong. It affects the just and the unjust, the deserving and the undeserving.

And here's something else you need to know up front. The workplace is a battleground. As believers in the workplace, we are citizens of God's Kingdom in a war that has two fronts—the spiritual realm and the natural realm where we live day to day.

SEE JOB SEEKER'S TIP #1: *"Why Are You Unemployed?"*

The two forces competing for this territory are the Kingdom of God and the kingdom of this world, and since we are in the world, we're behind enemy lines! All believers in the workforce are in this battle whether they like it or not. We could call ourselves soldiers, but as C.S. Lewis pointed out, we're more like *saboteurs.*[3]

You might think you're on the sidelines in this great battle, but make no mistake, as a follower of Jesus Christ engaged in "sabotage," you have not gone unnoticed by the "powers and principalities" of this world. You must stay in the battle, taking great care not to be compromised, corrupted or neutralized.

There are many ways this can happen. Your Christian witness can be compromised in the workplace if you fail to perform with the utmost integrity at all times. You can be seduced by get-rich-quick promises and be corrupted by material wealth that becomes an idol. You can even try to stay too long in a position that is no longer right for you. In a season of unemployment, you can be rendered ineffective by an attitude of defeat. Whether you're unemployed or your career is soaring, you can easily be taken out of action at a moment's notice if you don't stay closely connected to *the One who holds the victory.*

The main thrust of this book deals with unemployment, because a season of joblessness can be a serious threat to your mission. It can cause financial crisis, marital strife, depression and anxiety. If that's where you find yourself, we need to get you back in the war in a position of strength and confidence. You'll quickly discover, however, that the world doesn't want you to be a visible, prosperous witness in the workplace. That makes you dangerous. And that's exactly what God wants you to be—dangerous to the world. He also has a battle plan to equip you so that you can fight effectively and be victorious.

---

3. C.S. Lewis: *"Christianity is the story of how the rightful King has landed, you might say in disguise, and is calling us all to take part in His great campaign of sabotage."* Mere Christianity, pg. 51. (Chapter–The Invasion), First Touchstone Edition, 1996.

I've been asked by many believers if there is a way to opt out of this war. They want to skip the spiritual part and just do a regular job search. Sorry. The moment you chose to follow Jesus as your Lord and Savior, you chose sides. Moreover, the battle you'll be fighting is not only all around you, it is *within you* too.

...That's exactly what God wants you to be—dangerous to the world.

You see, work is matter of the heart. Each of us has to decide, sooner or later (I hope sooner!), whether we will give ourselves and our work lives to the will of God or whether we will keep fighting to stay in charge. For far too long many Christians have been allowed to believe that work is in a life compartment separate from God. Many have thought that God had no interest in their work as long as they performed it with integrity. You may have seen the popular graphic of a wheel showing religion, work, family, etc. as distinct pieces in the pie of life. I'm here to tell you that is not an accurate depiction of reality.

Religion, insofar as it represents our relationship with God and His Church, is not one piece of life. It isn't even the centerpiece of life. Quite simply Jesus is Life, the whole of it. There is no aspect of life that stands apart from Him. Instead of trying to fit God into our busy lives, we should be trying to fit our entire lives into the perfect will of God.

In this process of learning about God's view of work, you will see how much the condition of your heart impacts your employment journey. If you never realized this before, I may have just added to your concerns about this whole work life experience so allow me to reassure you with these words:

> *"God, who began the good work within you, will continue his work until it is finally finished on the day when Christ Jesus returns"* (Philippians 1:6).

We can trust in God to bring us through the job search and every other work and life experience. We just need to understand what is really going on. Too many believers are clueless about this spiritual battle for their hearts and the workplace and it's hurting them at work, in their careers, and in the job search process. What's even more damaging is they don't realize there is a Kingdom battle strategy to guide us and a secret weapon available only to them.

> *"But since we belong to the day, let us be self-controlled, putting on faith and love as a breastplate, and the hope of salvation as a helmet. For God did not appoint us to suffer wrath but to receive salvation through our Lord Jesus Christ. He died for us so that, whether we are awake or asleep, we may live together with him. Therefore encourage one another and build each other up, just as in fact you are doing"* (1 Thessalonians 5:8-11 NIV).

It's time for every believer, especially job seekers, to realize that we carry within us the very One who has already won this war.

The battle going on in and around you probably appeared daunting, and even overwhelming, before I told you about its spiritual implications. If you're currently out of work, you probably feel like you've got your hands full already just managing your own life and conducting your job search. You might want to stay focused on your personal situation and figure out how to get back to work as soon as possible without worrying about your spiritual condition or the workplace. Don't worry—both objectives, yours and the Kingdom's—can be achieved at the same time using exactly the same tactics. To go a step further, the unemployment and work challenges you face right now might also be the very preparation process that will equip you to help others who will experience this in the future. You will be able to share how God used this experience to make you stronger as you advanced with His direction.

It won't be easy—far from it. You've probably taken a few hits already. But never forget that the main battle has already been fought and won by our side through Jesus Christ.

> *"I also pray that you will understand the incredible greatness of God's power for us who believe him. This is the same mighty power that raised Christ from the dead and seated him in the place of honor at God's right hand in the heavenly realms. Now he is far above any ruler or authority or power or leader or anything else—not only in this world but also in the world to come. God has put all things under the authority of Christ and has made him head over all things for the benefit of the church. And the church is his body; it is made full and complete by Christ, who fills all things everywhere with himself"* (Ephesians 1:19-24).

You face a world that might seem overwhelming, but you have Christ on your side, and God has *"given Him the name which is above every name, that at the name of Jesus every knee should bow, of those in heaven, and of those on earth, and of those under the earth"* (Philippians 2:9-11 NKJV). The name of Jesus is the most powerful weapon that has ever existed!

Oh, you'll know you're in a fight, but you take into battle God's promise that *"no weapon formed against you shall prosper"* (Isaiah 54:17 NKJV).

Now, here's where you have to take another big leap of faith. Believe that God plans to use any and every experience of unemployment to bless and equip you. Your present situation is just like that of Joseph who was sold into slavery by his brothers. Years later he told them, "*You meant evil against me; but God meant it for good*" (Genesis 50:20 NKJV). There's nothing in your life that is a surprise or challenge to our God. Joseph recognized that God has the final say in everything affecting His children. God never changes. He's still in the business of turning circumstances to our benefit. So, just as He did with Joseph, He will lead you in triumph if you stick close to Him.

So what can you expect from a time out of work? Expect to be *transformed* as you allow God to have His way. I'm a mother of three and my oldest, a son, announced his intention to enlist in the Navy the day after the 9/11 tragedy. Shortly thereafter he packed up and went off to the Great Lakes Naval Training Center near Chicago. Thirteen weeks later I went to his graduation ceremony marking the end of boot camp. I was stunned at the transformation that had taken place in that time. Our time apart had seemed long to my son as he went through his training, but it seemed short to me in light of the dramatic changes I observed in him. Before me was a tall, confident man with a conviction about his life's purpose and a commitment to execute his assignment with excellence. Boot camp can do that to a person—testing, pushing, demanding and expecting performance levels never before attained by the individual.

Expect to be transformed as you allow God to have His way.

The experience of job loss or a sudden change in career direction can work similar powerful changes in your character and behavior. You might leave your job feeling shaky about what you have to offer and uncertain about what to do next. But by the time you hit the job market, you can be fully prepared and confident in your God-given talents and His ability to lead you through the process.

Confidence is just the start of the good news. James 1:3 tells us *"For you know that when your faith is tested, your endurance has a chance to grow. So let it grow, for when your endurance is fully developed, you will be perfect and complete, needing nothing."* Did you notice those last two words? Could it be that God wants to get you to a place where you really "need nothing" because you have His presence in you?

In my years of workplace ministry I've seen the love the Father has for His working children. I've discovered that He also has five special blessings or promises for every job seeker. I urge you to take Him up on every one of them. At the same time, you need to know that God will not force them upon you and there is a price to be paid if you choose to receive them. You must agree to place the Lord alone on the throne of your life, for He will not share that position with any other.

If you're having difficulty accepting that God wants your *unemployment* to be a wonderful, life-transforming experience, don't worry, you're not alone. Few believers find it easy to accept this, at least right away. The key is to understand that God doesn't view unemployment like we do. He doesn't see it as a gap on your resume. To Him, you're never really "out of a job."

Maybe this will help. Too often, Christians use the term "Lord" loosely. It's not a name. It's a title and a position description. It's your Boss's position description: **Lord** – noun, a person who has authority, control, or power over others; a master, chief, or ruler.[4]

---

4. Dictionary.com

God is your real Boss and Employer, and you still work for Him even if you're "unemployed" by the world's definition. He has big plans and plenty of assignments for you. Your Boss doesn't think like you do. His ways are not your ways.[5] The Father doesn't view your unemployment as a curse but as an opportunity to reveal Himself and His will for you during your season away from the world's workplace.

God is your real Boss and Employer, and you still work for Him even if you're "unemployed" by the world's definition.

So the **first blessing** is nothing less than a deep, personal relationship with God Himself. He sees this time as an opportunity to get with you one-on-one through your prayers and time in His Word. He wants to have a more intimate relationship with you. Imagine that—the Almighty, Creator of All, loves you and desires to be in fellowship with you! I'm going to park on this blessing for a while because it is far and away the most important of all and the prerequisite for receiving the four unemployment blessings that follow.

I cannot skip over this in the assumption that every believer already has a personal relationship with God because I know far too many who do not. I've found that it is possible for believers to sit in church week after week, say their prayers regularly, and try to live as God would desire, all without a personal experience of the overwhelming love of Jesus Christ. God desires so much more

5. Isaiah 55:8, "'For my thoughts are not your thoughts, neither are your ways my ways,' declares the Lord."

than this. A season out of the workplace offers the opportunity to enter into this type of relationship. I cannot overemphasize the importance of seeking Him and fellowshipping with Him. This is how you will learn to recognize His voice, to hear His instructions for your life and experience His love for you. In John 14:21 Jesus tells us, *"He who has My commandments and keeps them, it is he who loves Me. And he who loves Me will be loved by My Father, and I will love him and manifest Myself to him"* (NKJV).

In this day of the counterfeit, with so many voices calling you to paths that will take you away from God's plan for your life, it is essential that you take Him up on His offer to reveal Himself to you. There are many who would tell you that you can go through the Bible like it's a buffet line, picking the promises you like and calling them into being, but don't be deceived. It is Jesus alone who speaks to you through His Word to give you guidance and instruction. It must only be Jesus, the Good Shepherd, who leads, not you nor anyone else with their "guaranteed formulas" for success in life. With your life tucked securely in His will, you will have all you'll ever need! This alone would be far more than enough. But, there's more…

You've already received the **second blessing**, although you may not know the full extent of it. God has already wired you with special gifts and talents according to His plan and purposes. He's only been waiting for the perfect time to lead you to discover your God-given design and to put it to work.

God has already wired you with special gifts and talents according to His plan and purposes.

When you were working, there was far less time to think about your gifts and talents. You might have been too busy to reflect on what you know, what you've learned, and what you'd like to do with your experience. With a little breathing space and some time out of the workplace, you can begin to see that you indeed are *"fearfully and wonderfully made"* (Psalm 139:14 NIV).

Having made us in His image, God then commanded us to love others as we love ourselves. He knew this would be tough. There is no lack of selfishness and self-love in this world, and we can trace its roots right back to that first bite of the forbidden fruit. The world is filled with messages about "looking out for number one" and "speaking up for yourself" and that's a serious problem. We are full of ourselves, whether we are proud, self-centered and cocky, or self-pitying victims of "low self-esteem." Either way, we are obsessed with ourselves and not at all thinking about others. But, with the indwelling Spirit of Christ we are given the freedom to get outside ourselves and truly love others.

...With the indwelling Spirit of Christ we are given the freedom to get outside ourselves and truly love others.

> *"Love has been perfected among us in this: that we may have boldness in the day of judgment; because as He is, so are we in this world"* (1 John 4:17 NKJV).

Discovering that you are created to be like Jesus, designed in the image of God and perfectly and completely loved by God enables you to stop thinking about yourself (what could be more painful?) and begin loving others more fully. You'll be amazed at the joy you'll experience when you're set free from self-focus and self-protection and...well, self! This brings us to the **third blessing** of unemployment, enhancing and enriching our relationships with others.

SEE JOB SEEKER'S TIP #2: *"Prepare Your References"*

Many of us have experienced the stress of finding time for work, family and friends. I was a single mom for a number of years, and I constantly felt guilty about neglecting my children and my friends because of the hours I put into my work. I was always wishing that I had more time for the people I loved and more energy for the time I had with them. I'm sure you've had similar feelings.

A season of unemployment makes more relationship time possible. You still have to put in the hours required for job searching or working on the projects and assignments you find to do, but you have more flexibility to take a break and read a story to your toddler, to volunteer your time and gifts, or to meet a friend for coffee between appointments. Being of service to others, as God leads, is as important in a time of unemployment as it is when working.

Keeping focused on your marital relationship is especially important for couples in times of change and transition as well. It's so easy to fight over money and other stresses if you allow it to happen. There is a simple technique to avoid fighting with your spouse. The minute you sense a skirmish coming on, simply pray together—earnestly and deeply—for peace and understanding. It's impossible to fight and pray at the same time!

A season away from the workplace may be the perfect opportunity to rebuild important relationships too. I remember one job seeker who had been struggling with his teenage son. When the man lost his job, he finally had the time to show up at all of his son's ball games. He went out for pizza with the team after games and made time to help his son practice. Months later, when the man returned to work, he did so with a new, solid and loving relationship with his son.

A season away from the workplace may be the perfect opportunity to rebuild important relationships too.

The **fourth blessing** can also have an enormous impact on your life. God intends to free you from fear once and for all. Can you imagine a life without worry, concern, anxiety, fear, panic or terror? That's God's plan, and because it's so important, we'll spend a good bit of time learning how you can completely break free of fear.

I frequently ask job seekers if they would like to be free of fear, and they always say "Yes!" It's when I ask if they think it would be safe to stop worrying, and if they'd be willing to give it up, that their reaction changes. Somehow it seems that we just ought to worry a little. What would people think if you didn't panic from time to time about being without a job? If you don't express worry or anxiety, won't they think you're not taking your situation seriously? Do you really think God wants you to help Him by worrying things in for a landing?

Fear is so deeply entrenched in our lives that we think it's natural and that we just need to deal with it. Wrong! Remember, you still work for God and He didn't put fear in your "job description" and He didn't put it in you.

> *"For God has not given us a spirit of fear and timidity, but of power, love, and self-discipline"* (2 Timothy 1:7).

He doesn't want you to be afraid, and that's exactly why He's listed love as one of your duties—because it's the opposite of fear:

> *"There is no fear in love. But perfect love drives out fear"* (1 John 4:18).

Love and fear cannot coexist. Turn your attention to loving and serving others and you really will be free to walk in and out of future job interviews and work assignments fearlessly.

This brings us to the **fifth unemployment blessing**—a new job or work assignment. This was an exciting realization for me as I ministered to job seekers over the years. I learned that God wants your input as He opens up job opportunities for you. He doesn't have only one "right job" in mind. He isn't waiting for you to locate the only place that He's picked out. Instead, he makes Himself available to help you discover what you would most enjoy doing with your gifts and talents. He's looking for a full partnership with you.

Solomon, arguably the wisest man who ever lived, put it like this: *"I know that there is nothing better for men than to be happy and do good while they live. That everyone may eat and drink, and find satisfaction in all his toil—this is the gift of God"* (Ecclesiastes 3:12 NIV).

God wants your work to be deeply satisfying and this will only happen when you walk in partnership with Him and submit to His plan for your life. He can open all the necessary doors once you decide together how you'd like to put your gifts and talents to work for His purposes. You are a child of the Sovereign King. And, if it is His will, He is capable of placing you in any business or organization, in any location.

Of course it might take more than a few career discussions with Him to figure out where you'd like to work and how you'd like to contribute to the Kingdom. You may have to let go of some seriously wrong priorities and desires. Remember, you were designed for Kingdom work, not striving for a bigger house, a shinier car, or a more impressive title. It should be the goal of every believer to leave the footprint of Christ in the places they work and live.

If you don't know how you'd like to do this, ask God for guidance. He has known this about you since the beginning of time. *"For we are His workmanship, created in Christ Jesus for good works, which God prepared beforehand that we should walk in them"* (Ephesians 2:10 NKJV).

Once you're clear about this, you'll discover that He's gone before you to prepare a perfect place and to make sure the door is open to receive you. Sometimes you will have to go through a series of assignments to build toward your desired goal. Other times, your very next job will be the one that satisfies your deepest longings. But once you realize that your Father, the King, is on the journey with you, none of that will matter. He's got your back and you're going to be just fine. *"If God is for us, who can be against us?"* (Romans 8:31 NIV).

Let me stop here to make an important point. There is no promise that your journey will be easy. In fact, to do it right, making yourself completely open to receive all that God has for you, will require everything you've got. Even then you'll need the supernatural empowerment of God to get the job done. But just imagine what it will be like to end your season of unemployment or career change stronger, wiser and more spiritually connected to God than when you started. Wouldn't that qualify as "more than you could ask or think?"

"Now to him who is able to do immeasurably more than all we ask or imagine, according to his power that is at work within us" (Ephesians 3:20 NIV).

The key is in the phrase "*his power that is at work within us.*" As a believer, Christ is in you. Your job search is the perfect opportunity for Him to show you just how powerful He is—in and through you!

Now the question is, how exactly do you receive the five blessings that God promises during your season of unemployment? Here's just a hint of what's to come:

> *"And so I tell you, keep on asking, and you will receive what you ask for. Keep on seeking, and you will find. Keep on knocking, and the door will be opened to you. For everyone who asks, receives. Everyone who seeks, finds. And to everyone who knocks, the door will be opened"* (Luke 11:9-10).

In the chapters ahead, you'll learn how to do just that—ask, seek and knock. I have personally experienced or witnessed in the lives of other believers everything I will share with you. More importantly, everything will be backed up by the Word of God. I have also inserted a few Job Seeker Tips at the end of each chapter. These cover some critical behaviors that seem to pose particular difficulty for job seekers. I offer them to demonstrate how God's Word can be applied to practical, everyday situations in a way that will make a tangible and positive difference.

So put your faith in God to work. Keep reading with an open heart and mind, and you'll find what He has for you. The next step is to learn more about your current situation and what God has to say about it.

CHAPTER ONE

1. What causes unemployment and who can be affected by it?

2. Who is really in control of the workplace?

3. Why might an atheist have a job and a believer be unemployed?

4. How does God want you to use a season of unemployment?

5. How important are openness and expectation to receiving the five blessings of unemployment?

6. List the five blessings of unemployment:

JOB SEEKER'S TIP #1 Why Are You Unemployed?

There's no need to be concerned about this question, but there is a need to prepare for it. Without preparation there's danger of over-talking, sharing too much emotion, or simply missing the desired mark. Your goal is to be completely truthful and as brief as possible.

1. ***Be positive.*** State what is good about this change and why you are looking forward to it.

2. ***Keep it simple, clear and direct.*** Avoid jargon and fancy prose.

3. ***Be brief—no more than 5-6 sentences.*** Too much explanation and you'll sound defensive.

4. ***Give a good reason for the change,*** and avoid clichés. There are many reasons for changing positions, and the truth, presented comfortably, is always the best response. Here are some possibilities:

    - ***Layoff (when more than one is impacted), downsizing***
    - ***Reorganization, company relocation, merger, acquisition***
    - ***Limited opportunity for growth, blocked career path, no promotion from within***
    - ***Management changes, changes in company direction or philosophy (be prepared to explain it)***
    - ***Personality conflict, unable to support management decisions***

- ***Mistake or error on your part***
- ***Desire for new challenges, increased responsibility, change in personal direction.***

Practice saying it out loud and get feedback from a professional you trust.

Examples:

"I was affected by a layoff that impacted 10% of the workforce at my past company. I'm viewing this as an opportunity to use my operational background to get into healthcare, which is something I've always wanted to do."

"I was released for excessive absenteeism. I made the mistake of trying to manage a personal health issue by myself instead of arranging for support. I missed more days than I should have, and I understand why the company had to let me go. So I've learned from this mistake, and I'm committed to being on the job from now on."

JOB SEEKER'S TIP #2 Prepare Your References

Proverbs 15:23 states, *"Everyone enjoys a fitting reply; it is wonderful to say the right thing at the right time!"* You can arrange for those "fitting replies" to happen by effectively preparing your references.

1. ***Select your references.*** Always include past supervisors, a couple of coworkers, and two other professionals who know you well.

2. ***Determine the skills and attributes*** you want to highlight—in general or specifically targeted to an open position. Decide which references have seen you demonstrating those attributes.

3. ***Call your references personally.*** Ask permission to use them. Then ask each one to emphasize specific attributes when speaking to prospective employers. Remind each reference of examples and situations when you demonstrated that attribute. Get their agreement.

4. ***Follow up the call*** with a thank you, your resume and a reminder note about the attributes they agreed to emphasize.

What if you are expecting a bad reference?

Remember the promise of Isaiah 54:17: *"But in that coming day no weapon turned against you will succeed. You will silence every voice raised up to accuse you. These benefits are enjoyed by the servants of the Lord; their vindication will come from me. I, the Lord, have spoken!"*

Pray for the person, first and foremost. Usually, this is a former supervisor. Make sure there is no offense or resentment in your heart. Forgive the individual completely. Get God's help with this if you're struggling here.

Call the reference personally and ask what will be said about:

- ***Your reason for leaving***
- ***Would the reference rehire you? Why or why not?***
- ***Your strengths and weaknesses***

Write down the responses you receive and review what you heard by summarizing it aloud with the reference on the spot so there is no later confusion. Don't argue or defend yourself.

Close the conversation by expressing your desire to be professional. State that you value the experience you had and what you learned in your work with this person. Commit that you will speak positively about him/her and your former organization. Ask for the same.

When the interviewer asks for references, mention your concern about this specific reference. Share what the person said to you, in exact quotes. Offer equal and better references to counteract this one.

Important: Never just hope the bad reference won't happen. Prepare for it so the interviewer won't be surprised.

CHAPTER 2

GOOD NEWS

"For I know the plans I have for you," says the Lord. "They are plans for good and not for disaster, to give you a future and a hope."

– Jeremiah 29:11

"I have come that they may have life and have it more abundantly."

– John 10:10

Even if you're completely satisfied with your current position and not planning any immediate job or career change, you still need to read this chapter. The sad truth is, we all know people (probably several) who've been laid off and others who may have jobs but hate them. You'll be able to counsel and support them far more effectively with the information that follows. Also, at any time, *you* could go through a reorganization, a change of duties, a new boss, or even the loss of your job. So please read on with that in mind.

Let's go back to the question "Why me?" Earlier I said that this wasn't a particularly useful question, but it comes up too often to ignore. The question is really asking "What did I do to deserve this?" or "Why did God do this terrible thing to me?" or both. The answers are, "You didn't," and "God didn't."

Whether you contributed, knowingly or unknowingly, to becoming unemployed doesn't really matter. The truth is we rarely get what we deserve, good or bad, so trying to pin any circumstance in your life to a single cause is fruitless. And, as for attributing an attack on you to the Father who loves you best? Well, that's just silly.

In this battle for the workplace, the Enemy would like nothing better than for you to blame God for your job loss and troubles. Don't fall into that trap. We live in a fallen world, and there are any number of reasons why you may have lost your job, your business, and even your dreams through no fault of your own. In fact, you may have lost your job or business precisely because you follow Jesus. If you recall the Sermon on the Mount, Jesus told His disciples that this might happen and what God would do as a result. "*What blessings await you when people hate you and exclude you and mock you and curse you as evil because you follow the Son of Man. When that happens, be happy! Yes, leap for joy! For a great reward awaits you in heaven*" (Luke 6:22-23).

Even if you were willfully deficient in your work, don't dwell on it. Sincerely confess it to God, repent and go on.

Dwelling on these past events is simply a distraction from the job at hand, which is to get going on your job search.

As for trying to find some hidden mistake you may have made, or things you should have done differently in your prior job, don't bother. Even if you could find a reason for the loss of your job or business, it wouldn't change things. Dwelling on these past events is simply a distraction from the job at hand, which is to get going on your job search.

Now, there may be one exception to this rule. If you've lost a business and intend to one day launch another, reflecting on best practices and engaging in *constructive* self-critique is helpful—but not just yet. That work is best done after you've received some of the blessings of unemployment and you are emotionally stable.

I trust this insight will enable you to stop endlessly chasing down rabbit trails in your mind. Hopefully, it will also help you resist blaming others (who may not have had anything to do with your situation) or engaging in self-condemnation or paranoia. That will only add to the shock and loss you feel and it won't help. If you must blame someone, blame the Enemy who loves to take advantage of you in a time of weakness. But remember, your focus needs only to be on how to recover your footing and strength and get back into the workforce.

Knowing all this, you may be asking how God figures into the situation. As I said before, God didn't do any terrible thing to you. God doesn't cause His children harm—ever! It's not in His character and it's not in the Word. Think about this scripture: *"Or what man is there among you who, if his son asks for bread, will give him a stone?"* (Matthew 7:9 NKJV) And yet we imagine that God would take away our jobs and walk away as we struggle. His Word clearly states that He *"will never leave you nor forsake you"* (Hebrews 13:5 NKJV).

Each time I've made that statement I've heard the objections. "What about the things He did to the Israelites in the Old Testament?" Okay, let's look at the way God interacted with His people in the Old Testament.

We know that Old Testament believers were not, in themselves, righteous. They had to make sacrifices and rely on the intercession of their priests to obtain God's grace and mercy. They were commanded to follow the Law and to seek forgiveness continuously in order to maintain a right standing with God. Often they failed. When they repented, cried out for mercy and sought to obey, they were forgiven. As they walked in obedience, they were outrageously blessed. Every time they turned away from God and openly rebelled, they experienced the very negative consequences of their choice. But, never forget, they had the choice to trust God and to obey Him. It was their rebellion that brought their troubles, not their God.

Now let's look at the new covenant we have as New Testament believers in Christ Jesus, the *"Mediator of a better covenant which was established on better promises"* (Hebrews 8:6 NKJV). It is absolutely true that Jesus took the entire wrath of God upon Himself for our sake. The price for our unrighteousness has been paid, in full and for all time. We have been forgiven of all our sins—past, present and future! We were made righteous in Christ Jesus. Because of Jesus, we are now positioned to receive God's entire blessing and none of His righteous anger. Once again a choice has been given to the people of God. We can receive the gift of His righteousness and walk in obedience to His commands or we too can experience the consequences of turning away from the Light.

This brings us to chastening, the discipline of God. In the words of Charles Spurgeon, a renowned Christian preacher, "The rod of chastisement must rest upon us in our measure, but it worketh for us the comfortable fruits of righteousness; and therefore by the aid of the divine Comforter, we, the 'people saved of the Lord,' will joy in the God of our salvation." So, no question about it, God corrects us and sometimes that hurts. But He does so as a loving Father. Years ago I heard a comedian talk about his father. He said that every night his dad would come home from work, line up all of his children and give each one a big smack. As he did this he would say, "I may not know what this is for, but you do!" Some of us seem to think God would behave like that. He doesn't. He isn't going to rise up suddenly one day and knock you flat and leave you wondering what you've done wrong.

If God has ever convicted you about a sinful behavior that He wants you to stop, you know what I mean. There's no surprise element to it—no wrath, no anger, no attack—just a very clear message that you need to repent and walk another way. When God convicts, I doubt that anyone would ask "Why?" because there is no confusion in His word to us. If we ignore His direction, however, we will walk ourselves into greater sin and danger. This bad choice can lead to consequences that would have been completely avoided had we heeded His first call to correction.

God certainly may use this season of unemployment to show believers where they have turned away from His word and to convict them of sinful behaviors. Don't be surprised if you discover, in your job search process, that you had work behaviors that were not pleasing to God and now He's helping you to leave them in the past. Through His correction He will keep you from walking back into bondage to world systems. *"If you are not disciplined (and everyone undergoes discipline) then you are illegitimate children not true sons. Moreover, we have all had human fathers who disciplined us and we respected them for it. How much more should we submit to the Father of our spirits and live! Our fathers disciplined us for a little while as they thought best; but God disciplines us for our good, that we may share in his holiness. No discipline seems pleasant at the time, but painful. Later on, however, it produces a harvest of righteousness and peace for those who*

Through His correction He will keep you from walking back into bondage to world systems.

have been trained by it" (Hebrews 12:8-12 NIV). So whenever this happens to us we should be grateful for it. Be willing to learn what you need to from the lesson and move on.

Finally, and best of all, God offers us the opportunity to judge ourselves.[6] As we spend more time in His presence we will learn to be like Him. Then we'll be able to catch ourselves when we sin or wander away. We will be able to come to Him without chastisement, repent, receive His forgiveness and, with the help of the Holy Spirit, walk in freedom from sin.

In this time of transition, I would suggest that where there is confusion, shock and fear, you'll find the Enemy, probably whispering in your ear, telling you it's not right and that God has forgotten or turned upon you. And that would be a lie. For wherever there is humility and true repentance—love, comfort, strength and wisdom rush in and that's where you'll find God! As you go forth into the workplace to find your next position, go with the clear understanding that God is good and only good. It's imperative to trust Him with your job search, your career, and your life. You can't go forward in confidence and strength if you don't know what you've been given in Christ and Who is fighting alongside you.

The Gospel, or good news, is that God loves you and has your highest and best in mind for you always. If He steps in to save you, it is for your good. If He moves you, it's for your good. And, if He corrects you, it is for your good. Every one of these situations may feel uncomfortable; you might not understand what you're experiencing, but you can trust the One who loves you perfectly to carry you through the transition. And, for even more good news, if through sin or carelessness you caused your situation or you fell

---

6. *"But if we judged ourselves, we would not come under judgment"* (1 Corinthians 11:31 NIV).

prey to a snare of the Enemy, God is still right there with you. Your loving Father will always have you in His righteous hands. Period.

This spiritual discussion may appear to have nothing to do with unemployment, but it does. It's critical that you understand the character of God, where you, as His redeemed child, stand with Him, and the absolute power of the completed work of Jesus Christ. You have to know who you're fighting with and who you're fighting against. The really good news of our situation is that God is with you; He's on your side! What you can learn from the Old Testament is this—the God who delivered the children of Israel by splitting open the Red Sea is our present-day God. The God who, to ensure victory for His children, unleashed angelic forces in battle, made the sun stand still for a day, and leveled a walled city, is our same God. Your Father is ready and able to lead you to victory over your circumstances.

Your Father is ready and able to lead you to victory over your circumstances.

This does raise one more question, however. Why did He allow this to happen? After all, God is all-powerful and all-knowing. He could have prevented your job loss, but He didn't. He saw it coming, so why didn't He keep it from happening?

That's the million-dollar question and here's what I can tell you. Once again it comes back to that same matter of choice that we discussed earlier. This time we're not talking about your choice but *mankind's* choice. When God made man He did so in His image and likeness. He gave man dominion over all the earth and He gave man free will. In Genesis 1:26-28 we see that His intention was to turn the world over to us and have us rule here as He does in heaven. We all know the story of man's disobedience and the entrance of sin into the world. It's pretty obvious that the world is no longer a garden and God's love is not the ruling force here. There are many people willfully turning their backs on God every day and choosing to live in sin and disobedience. Countless others have never heard of God or considered His existence. There are also many, including believers, who love God but do not know how to walk in the victory of Jesus Christ. So bad things continue to happen to good people in this fallen world.

Don't misunderstand. God is most certainly sovereign. It simply means that He honors His decision to give mankind choices, even when they are clearly not what He would desire for us. For our sake, though, He has established higher spiritual laws that still govern heaven and earth. Obedience to the principles of His Kingdom economy will always give you spiritual victory no matter what the world throws at you. He has made a way for you to walk victoriously in this world but you have to follow His road map to accomplish it.

As a job seeker, you are always free to walk in the way of the Spirit or to continue in the way of the world. You can choose to obey God's law, the Spirit of life, or to abide by the world's law of sin and death. "*For the law of the Spirit of life in Christ Jesus has made me free from the law of sin and death*" (Romans 8:2 NKJV). There's no question about the right choice for a successful job search, is there?

God's way is clearly the superior law. We'll go into this in much greater depth when we talk about your citizenship in the Kingdom of God. For now, just understand that you are in constant danger of submitting to the laws of this world until you learn to fully walk with Christ.

Where does this leave you? Should you accept that the world can knock you out of the workplace and God can do nothing about it? Not at all! The Word of God is very clear about this. *"And we know that all things work together for good to those who love God, to those who are called according to His purpose"* (Romans 8:28 NKJV).

That same chapter ends with this powerful declaration:

> *"Yet in all these things we are more than conquerors through Him who loved us. For I am persuaded that neither death nor life, nor angels nor principalities nor powers, nor things present nor things to come, nor height nor depth, nor any other created thing, shall be able to separate us from the love of God which is in Christ Jesus our Lord"* (Romans 8:37-39 NKJV).

You have to realize that God's view of unemployment differs sharply from the world's. Remember, unemployment is a neutral event. It's not a guaranteed disaster despite what the world would have you believe. Rather, unemployment has the potential to be an adventure with the promise of treasure. *"Fear not, for I am with you. Be not dismayed, for I am your God. I will strengthen you, Yes, I will help you, I will uphold you with my righteous right hand"* (Isaiah 41:10 NKJV). We've already seen how God can use this time to correct something that might have been holding us back and to create His character in us. Those are two valuable treasures right there.

Given that He is not surprised at your situation and is not remotely challenged by it, He may actually have a wonderful transformation in store for you. I know it's a challenge to imagine that a season of unemployment or miserable misemployment can be turned into something good. In fact, right now you might be willing to settle for any job that pays at least what you were making. Guess what? That's just not good enough for God! He has something else in mind.

I've seen the awesome outcomes that God can achieve in seasons of unemployment. He is, without a doubt, the author of the world's greatest turnaround strategies. I think God has a fine old time turning the world's worst attacks into your greatest blessings. Even if the Enemy himself were attacking you, remember, *"For this purpose the Son of God was manifested, that He might destroy the works of the devil"* (1 John 3:8 NKJV).

I told you earlier that God has five things He'd like to accomplish while you're "on the sidelines." He desires (1) to build a stronger relationship with you; (2) to convince you that you were fearfully and wonderfully made with special gifts and talents; (3) to improve your capacity to love others; (4) to free you from fear; and (5) to lead you into your next assignment.

So can He do all that? What do you think? When God promised Abraham and Sarah a child in their old age, Sarah doubted His ability. God responded by asking, *"Is anything too hard for the Lord?"* (Genesis 18:14). Now He's asking you that question. Is your present situation too big for Him to handle? Of course not!

Let's take a look at His top turnaround strategies and see if He might not be formulating one of these for you right now.

Let's call the first turnaround "From Wrecked to Restored." If you've been overworked, exhausted, stressed and pressured in your job, He gives you rest and restoration. *"Come to me, all of you who are weary and carry heavy burdens, and I will give you rest"* (Matthew 11:28).

Bodies, minds and emotions are healed in this transformation. Sometimes work just takes over our lives and we lose sight of our true priorities. That's when time out of the workplace can restore balance and rescue relationships.

Robert had just started his time out of work and joined my small group when his son decided, for the first time, to skip school with a bunch of buddies.[7] Robert got the call from the police station telling him to pick up his son. That may not sound like a blessing but it was. As he tells it, he was right there to see the first warning sign that his son needed more attention and more direction. Robert was able to deal with the sort of issue he'd always pushed off on his wife. With God's help, he was able to turn the situation around.

There are times when God picks up the pieces of a shattered life and puts them back together. Amanda lost her job just when her fiancé told her he was in love with someone else. At that exact same time her roommate suddenly kicked her out so a boyfriend could move in. How's that for a disaster? No relationship, no job and no home. Amanda was devastated. I met her the day she lost her home and after telling me her story through her tears, she declared that she was trusting God and that she believed He would care for her as He had always done.

That very afternoon that she found herself without a home, a friend connected her with a family needing a house sitter. Instantly, Amanda had a private room with bath and her meals were provided. As she got her health and peace of mind back, she was able to bless this family. When the time came that they no longer needed her, she landed a great job and was back on her feet.

Amanda would be the first to tell you it was all God's doing. She had no clue what she was going to do . . . then God stepped in to meet all of her needs. Now she has a better job than the one she lost and is profoundly relieved not to have married a man who couldn't be faithful.

---

7. Names may have been changed to protect the privacy of individuals. However, all of the stories are absolutely authentic!

The second turnaround is "From Stuck to Start-up." If you've gotten into a dead-end job or a skill set that is no longer marketable, God can make a way to retool and redirect you.

As a consultant, I did outplacement seminars for 200 employees taking early retirement from a major computer company. They weren't happy about leaving. Most felt they were being forced out of the company. And yet, in every seminar, when I asked the participants how long it had been since they'd been happy in their jobs and done work they enjoyed, the majority said it had been more than a decade! Don't you think that's tragic?

I had the chance to minister to some of these people and see them launch new businesses—like pet grooming, jewelry making, and massage therapy, of all things. Their severance packages helped them to do things they had only dreamed about before. Initially they were angry about losing their jobs, but many ended up truly glad that their other careers had ended.

There was a man at our church who lost his high paying, managerial position in banking. When he couldn't find a job, he decided to work at the church and help build a new school. As he worked on its construction, God kept providing part-time jobs and other ways to keep his family supported. Over time, he learned more and more about construction and moved into the role of general contractor for the church project. By the time the building was completed, two years later, this man had been completely retooled for a new career in construction. Today he is a very successful home builder. How's that for a business start-up strategy? It was as if God was saying, once again, *"I have appointed you for the very purpose of displaying my power in you and to spread my fame throughout the earth"* (Romans 9:17). This individual never envisioned himself with a future in the construction business, but God knew just how to accomplish a perfect career change so that he might prosper.

SEE JOB SEEKER'S TIP #3: "Project Boot Camp"

The third turnaround is "From Busy to Blessing." How many times have you said, "I wish I had time to . . . ?" Projects come up but we can't get to them because we're working. Friends and family need us but we're unavailable. Sometimes God lets us stay out of the workplace to give us time for a special project or personal need.

I met Raul a few years ago when he lost his job. He had also just learned that his brother was dying of cancer. Many people commented that this was too much for one person to bear, but that's not how Raul saw it. He was grateful for the precious time he was able to spend with his brother and that he was able to offer strength and support to his brother's family. Raul told our group that he praised God for allowing him this time away from work. Within a few weeks of the funeral, he had a new job paying just what he had hoped to earn.

When you lay aside your work to be right where God wants you, you are always blessed. Isn't that what Jesus was saying to Martha? She was upset with her sister Mary for sitting at the feet of Jesus while she rushed about working. Jesus said *"There is only one thing worth being concerned about. Mary has discovered it, and it will not be taken away from her"* (Luke 10:42).

The final turnaround is "From Scrapped to Saved." It's easy for this intervention to go unnoticed. It's when God sees danger ahead of us and acts to get us out of danger. The harm is averted and we may never know that we were in danger.

Of course, there are some situations, like the Twin Tower tragedy of 9/11, where God's saving grace is very obvious. Think of the workers who had recently lost their jobs in the World Trade Center only to realize later they might have lost *their lives* had they still been employed there. I've talked to individuals who lost jobs and found new ones just before their former employers laid off even more workers. Imagine their relief to be safe in new jobs before all those other job seekers hit the streets. I met one person who lost his job and later found out that his former company went out of business, still owing paychecks to all the remaining workers. Psalm 121:7 promises us, *"The Lord will keep you from all harm—He will watch over your life"* (NIV). Your job loss might feel uncomfortable but it could be the very thing saving you from something much worse.

I've not only observed God's turnaround strategies; I've benefited from them. I had a very successful career at a large multinational corporation for a number of years. I was promoted four times in six years and had become the international staffing manager. My pay raises and salary adjustments had been far above the norm. Unfortunately, I reached a point where the work I was doing was no longer satisfying. I found myself caught up in endless meetings and administrative tasks rather than managing the actual staffing and hiring activities I really enjoyed. Still, the position paid well, so I ignored the nagging dissatisfaction and kept working. My situation would change soon anyway because I was getting married and looking forward to leaving work and starting a family with my new husband. So I figured I'd just ride out the job until that time.

But as the year drew to a close, I felt God telling me to leave the job. Unfortunately, I didn't obey. Instead, I explained to God that it wouldn't make sense to leave right then. If I waited until after the wedding, my children would have continuous benefits coverage. (Don't you love how we think we're telling God something

He doesn't already know?) I didn't hear any more from the Lord, so I assumed He and I agreed that I could keep my job for a while.

A few weeks later I was in my boss's office to brief him on a project when he abruptly closed the door and announced that the agenda for our meeting had changed. He informed me that effective immediately I was being asked to resign. The reason he gave for this sudden action made absolutely no sense to me. He cited an infraction that seemed insignificant. Apparently, months earlier, at the request of a senior manager, I had processed an invoice for an amount exceeding my approval authority. Please understand, the invoice itself was for a legitimate expense and not fabricated in any way. The error I made was merely that of unknowingly signing for an amount that was above my "limit." This was a complete surprise to me, because I had previously signed invoices over my limit without incident.

I explained that I hadn't realized I was doing something wrong and that I was never informed there was a problem. It didn't matter. I had the choice to resign or be fired. He took my building pass and keys, opened the door, and handed me off to a security guard. I was permitted into my office only to retrieve my purse, and then briskly escorted out the door to the parking garage. In less than twenty minutes my years of excellent performance with this company had been erased and I was marked as an "undesirable."

Alone in the parking garage, I sat in my car absolutely stunned and devastated. I cried out to God demanding to know why He allowed this to happen. In His infinite patience, God gently reminded me that He had directed me to leave months ago. Had I obeyed I would have avoided the pain I was now experiencing. So there I was—unemployed, shocked, deeply hurt, and embarrassed to the point of shame. If you've ever been in a situation like this, you know how the questions begin to swirl in your mind. What will people say about me? What will all my friends and coworkers think? How will I support my children? Who will ever hire me now that I have been fired? Who will believe me about what happened? I was shaking so badly with fear, anger and shame that I could hardly drive home.

One of the hardest things I ever had to do was to go back that weekend to clear out my things. Then I stayed for an hour and helped my former manager to transition my work and files, making sure that my leaving wouldn't negatively affect others. As I was leaving he thanked me and expressed his gratitude for the way I had handled the experience. Looking back this seemed such a small thing but by enabling me to do this God gave me a sense of victory over the situation.

My real purpose in sharing this story is to show you how insignificant unemployment is to God when He has something much, much better in mind for us. One year from that horrible day, I was the head of a successful consulting practice, doing work I really enjoyed. To make it happen, God used all of His turnaround strategies on my behalf! I give him all the glory and credit. I had little to do with my eventual turnaround. After I lost my job, I felt hopeless and helpless. I felt hurt by the treatment I had received and was clueless about how I could get out of the situation. Because I hadn't taken God up on His offer to save me, I got thrown on the scrap heap. But being "scrapped" and forced to leave that position was a blessing to me. I hadn't been happy there and was spending far too much time away from my children. It was time to move on but I had become too comfortable to go without a push!

God's next turnaround strategy for me was "Restoration." Years of long hours had turned me into a physical wreck. I had fueled my breakneck pace with chain smoking and a continuous infusion of coffee. Two herniated disks in my lower back kept me in constant pain. I was exhausted. I had been too busy to even ask for God's healing touch.

The first healing miracle happened my very first day out of work. God directed me to stop smoking and I did. I simply stopped and the habit was broken without any withdrawal effects! Time and time again I had tried to quit, using every available method, but with no success. Then, in one day, God freed me. I haven't had a cigarette in my mouth since that day.

A few weeks later I learned that our church had a Tuesday morning healing ministry, so I dragged myself to a service. I was hurting so badly I couldn't respond when the pastor told us to raise our hands to receive healing. The person seated next to me saw my struggle, grabbed my hand, and held it up for me. Like a lightning bolt, energy shot through my body from my head to my toes and my back was completely healed! Within a few weeks of losing my job, God delivered not one, but two, instantaneous healings to a person who never thought it could happen to her! Obviously, I would not have been in that weekday service if I hadn't been fired. Clearly God used my time out of work for healing and restoration.

As for turnaround strategy number three, after my termination, I didn't have a clue what to do with myself. I didn't feel like I could go back to work anywhere. How would I explain being fired? So I went to my church and volunteered to do whatever was needed. My high-powered career had afforded me no time for volunteering. Here was a chance to do something good while I figured out where to go next.

Given my corporate background, I thought the church would give me a leadership position or at least somehow use my education, experience, and expertise. Instead, I was assigned to greet people and handle the telephone switchboard. Now if you ask me, God has a quirky sense of humor! I'm what you might call "administratively challenged." However, while my new volunteer role was definitely not what I'd envisioned, it proved to be a wonderful plan. That assignment allowed me to meet all the pastors, staff and leaders in this huge church and fully connect with its ministries. It was here that my first job ministry was born with the support of many of the people I met as the volunteer receptionist. God moved me from Busy to Blessing, into a place where I could serve the body of Christ for years to come.

Now you'll see how God took me from Stuck to Start-up. I've told you I was clueless about what work to do next. I wanted to stay home and raise a family but our financial needs were too great. I would have to work somewhere. So I answered phones at my church, waited and worried my way through a pretty miserable summer. Little did I know what God had in store for me.

A former coworker tracked me down at the church and invited me to bid on a consulting project at her company. They were planning a major staffing project and she thought I was the right person to handle it. I landed that contract and the project was a success. Then I took on another big staffing project and it was also successful. My consulting career was launched. I ended the year making more money than ever before, and I was doing work that really made a difference in people's lives. Over 500 people got new jobs in those two staffing projects that God provided. What's more, I was also able to hire more than sixty-five contractors to help with those projects so the financial blessing spilled out onto all of them as well.

Looking back, I can now see that God used my so-called employment tragedy to accomplish every one of His transformations in me. I didn't see this at the time and I spent some pretty miserable months trying to get over what had happened. Still, there is no doubt that I came through in victory by God's grace and design. What a wonderful new course God set me on when my corporate career came crashing down around my ears!

Now it's time to get back to you and your situation. Can you see the hand of God in your circumstances yet? I promise you, He's right there. As surely as He blessed me and the countless others I have seen over the years, He is poised and ready to transform your situation too.

There is no power in heaven or on earth that can stop God if we'll bring Him into our situations. This has been the nature of God since the beginning of time. Look how David described God: "*Who forgives all your iniquities, Who heals all your diseases, Who redeems your life from destruction, Who crowns you with lovingkindness and tender mercies, Who satisfies your mouth with good things, So that your youth is renewed like the eagle's*" (Psalm 103:3-5).

That sure sounds like transformation to me. So don't rush back out into the job market without first spending time with God. Ask Him to reveal His plan for you. I know the urge is great to find another job quickly, but if you're like most people, you'll do yourself more harm than good if you launch yourself out there before God says you're ready.

...Don't rush back out into the job market without first spending time with God.

Let's talk about change for a moment. No matter how much you might like to skip this part, every person experiencing a significant life change will have to travel through a time of transition and grieving. Many job seekers are unaware of this, and they plunge out into the job market before they're ready.

You need to work through your emotions and get prepared before you can initiate a successful job search. It takes time to get organized for a new life. Much of what you took for granted is gone. You are now without a schedule, coworkers, workplace, job description, or purpose. God will help you sort all this out, but you have to set aside time to be with Him.

I've interviewed far too many people who moved into their job searches immediately and ended up falling completely apart in the interview. They had no idea what abilities they had to offer, nor could they clearly state what they wanted to do.

In the absence of a solid foundation, *fear* drives job seekers to desperation. They say things to prospective employers and networking contacts that they should never say. God's plan is much better. Jesus tells us "*Seek the Kingdom of God above all else, and live righteously, and he will give you everything you need*" (Matthew 6:33).

God wants to show believers His way of doing things. I promise you this, His is the way to go! We'll talk about the specific steps you can take to conduct an excellent and effective job search a little later. Just be assured that God has all the time and provisions you need. He'll keep you covered as you get your act together. To go into your job search without Him and without taking time for transition, preparation and guidance is just asking for trouble.

Wherever you are right now, evaluate your circumstances. Is it time for you to make a job or career change? If you're already out of the workplace, do you need time to physically recover from a tough work experience? Is there some situation or relationship in your life that needs your full attention? Have you been dreaming of something you'd like to accomplish for the Kingdom of God? Is there a new line of work that really seems to be calling to you? Pray about it. Ask God to show you how He wants you to spend your time as you prepare for your next assignment. He probably has placed some projects right under your nose. Work on those assignments, then trust Him to work his turnaround strategy for you.

You also need to consider yourself employed from now on. ***The truth is that you work for God Himself and you will never be out of work again.*** There is no end to the things that need to be accomplished for the Kingdom and you're the only one who can perform the assignments that have your name on them. God is fully prepared to compensate you for the work you do for Him. His rewards are eternal and more than enough and the assignments He gives will bless you while you're completing them.

However, God is not obligated to pay for work He didn't assign. So spend time with Him to see what turnarounds He has in mind for you. As you discover what assignments God has for you while you're out of the workplace, take them on without fear. Don't worry about doing everything perfectly. It's enough simply to act in obedience. You'll receive further direction from God as needed. You are now in a boot camp just like the one we spoke about earlier, and God's about to turn your situation around!

CHAPTER TWO

1. Does God use unemployment as a punishment? How can you be sure about this?

2. List and describe God's turnaround strategies.

3. Which of these strategies applies to you right now? How?

4. Describe a time when a "tragedy" in your life turned out to be a blessing.

5. How important is it to deal with the normal emotional aspects of change before beginning the job search process? Why?

6. Why is it important to obey God's direction in your life?

JOB SEEKER'S TIP #3 Project Boot Camp

There are plenty of things that you won't be able to control during your job search. Don't make the mistake of thinking that your whole life is out of your control. You need to create a project plan for yourself and stick to it. Every night, as you reflect on your day, make sure you have accomplished things that you feel good about.

SET YOUR GOALS

Make your job search commitments:

- ***Set up your work space.***
- ***Plan the hours you'll spend every day organizing and implementing your job search activities.***

Allow for restoration:

- ***Get your body in order. Exercise, eat healthy foods, drink water and sleep.***
- ***Get your relationships in order. Spend time with loved ones, write letters, visit, and listen. Make connections with your spouse and children.***
- ***Get your house in order. Clean out closets, attics, basements and garages. (Give away whatever you can.) Organize your files. Complete all those tasks you never had time for!***

Be willing to do a start-up:

- ***Volunteer somewhere and make a difference.***
- ***Follow your heart.***
- ***Investigate the type of work you've dreamed about. What's required and how can you prepare for it?***
- ***Learn new skills. Take a class, go to seminars, get busy reading and researching so you'll go back to work with more than you had when you left.***
- ***Put your hobby to work. Sell your products/services or give them away. Get some giving-seed in the ground so God can bring a harvest.***

Be a blessing:

- ***What church project needs your gifts and talents?***
- ***What friend or family member needs your support?***
- ***Who can you bless with your presence and abilities?***

Plan your days:

Set a daily schedule and stick to it (structure)

- ***Start with God's Word and prayer***
- ***Build in exercise and rest (but don't turn the TV on during the day!)***

Make progress on your job search

- ***Prepare your presentation materials (references, resume, interview responses)***
- ***Research the marketplace***
- ***Generate leads and make networking calls***
- ***Interview and follow up***

Accomplish your project goals

- *Get some part of your projects completed every day*
- *Work as hard and as fast as you can. You don't know how soon you'll be going back to work.*

Track your progress:

- *Make yourself accountable to someone other than your spouse!*
- *Determine to complete your projects before you start a new job.*

JOB SEEKER'S TIP #4 *Take Time for Transition*

Change always triggers a time of adjustment. Whether we consider the change to be good or bad, we'll still experience a whole set of emotions as we transition into a new experience and leave the past behind. If you plan for the feelings that accompany this adjustment, they won't surprise or overwhelm you.

During the transition you'll be traveling through three distinct phases. Read each description to locate where you are right now and then take the actions that will help you move on.

Don't let anyone tell you that this is abnormal, that you are not okay, or that things will always be like this. Transition is temporary. If you'll keep moving you'll overcome the Enemy's plan to get you to quit and give up.

PHASE ONE – WHAT HAVE I LOST? WHAT JUST ENDED?

How it feels and what it looks like:

- ***Shock***
- ***Anger***
- ***Sadness***
- ***Stress***
- ***Panic***
- ***Loss***
- ***Betrayal***
- ***Grief***
- ***Impossibility***
- ***Overwhelming***

What you need to move forward:

Patience; empathy (not sympathy!) from other believers; and one good listener who will validate your worth and assure you that you are still valuable.

PHASE TWO - WHAT'S GOING ON? WHAT DO I DO NOW?

How it feels and what it looks like:

- *Chaotic*
- *Confusion*
- *Insecure*
- *Frustrating*
- *Depression*
- *Stressful*
- *Exhausting*
- *Lonely*
- *Creative*
- *Searching*

What you need to move forward:

Structure/schedule; information and training; and communication—lots of it.

PHASE THREE - HOW CAN I DO WHAT I WANT TO DO?

How it feels and what it looks like:

- *Hopeful*
- *Engaging*
- *Impatient*
- *Optimistic*
- *Stressful*
- *Exciting*
- *Motivated*
- *Willing*
- *Determined*
- *Anxious*

What you need to move forward:

Encouragement; practice opportunities; connections and resources.

CHAPTER 3

BREAK FREE

"Fear not, for I am with you; Be not dismayed, for I am your God. I will strengthen you, Yes, I will help you, I will uphold you with My righteous right hand."

– Isaiah 41:10 NKJV

"For God has not given us a spirit of fear, but of power and of love and of a sound mind."

– 2 Timothy 1:7 NKJV

Now, as God begins to turn your concept of unemployment or misemployment from tragedy to treasure hunt, we're going to shine a floodlight on fear. For far too long, believers have been rendered ineffective, if not completely paralyzed, by fear. But with the God of the Universe on our side, why would we be afraid of anything? The only fear we should have is the fear of God, certainly not of man. And that is a holy awe type of fear, not the sense you get when you're under attack.

Remember that you are behind enemy lines. The entire world system is against you and there is no place for you to comfortably fit in. You are at least a nuisance, if not an out-and-out threat with your Bible on display in your work station, asking for Sunday off, or insisting on absolute integrity in the marketplace. So you have a bull's eye on your back, and fear is the normal reaction when someone is shooting at you. But this is not a "normal" war and you are not a helpless target. You have been armed for this battle.

> *"For though we live in the world, we do not wage war as the world does. The weapons we fight with are not the weapons of the world. On the contrary, they have divine power to demolish strongholds. We demolish arguments and every pretension that sets itself up against the knowledge of God, and we take captive every thought to make it obedient to Christ"* (2 Corinthians 10:3-5 NIV).

You definitely have the ability to overcome every spiritual impediment—anything this world throws at you; Christ has promised it. With training you will avoid the world's traps, develop the ability to fight back, and even bring some light into this present darkness as you search for a new job or change careers.

I told you that God wants to deliver every job seeker from fear during a season of unemployment or employment transition preparation. He is ready to do this for you, if you allow Him. My advice is, don't wait another day. Just imagine how different things might have been if you had begun your work life on the solid foundation of God's career strategy, plan and processes. I know I could certainly have avoided a lot of pain and trauma. My hope is that I can share with you what I've learned so you'll be able to put it to good use immediately—whether you're in the workplace or temporarily out of it.

Here's thc bottom line—God has made a way for you to be completely fearless. That's His plan for your entire life, and a job search is no exception. When you learn to conquer fear, in all its forms, and bring the presence of God into your employment circumstances, you triumph. Sure, it's possible to limp through a job search (that's how I did it), but why not make the journey walking boldly in the strength and joy of the Lord?

So first, we're going to slam the door on fear. Then we'll uncover specific tactics used against believers who are job seeking and mount a defense against them. Finally, we'll train with our spiritual weapons of war and prepare to take back the workplace, one job at a time.

As I said before, we're in a war. We happen to live in the one, tiny spot in the entire universe that is in open rebellion against the Creator. *"And from the days of John the Baptist until now the kingdom of heaven suffers violence, and the violent take it by force"* (Matthew 11:12 NKJV).

Like it or not, you're a soldier, a spy or a saboteur in this war. You must come to see yourself as a loyalist fighting for the King. There are no neutral parties in this war. Many believers have been, and still are, unaware of the battle that rages around them. They're not prepared to go on the offensive, much less defend against it.

It's time to radically change your plan of attack. You must stop clinging to a bad job, thinking it's all you're able to do. You must never again go into the job market like a beggar hoping for a crumb of a job! You must learn to go forth confident that there's a great, new assignment out there with your name on it. But know that you're going to have to fight for it with a firm mental resolve.

Isaiah says it like this: *"Because the Sovereign Lord helps me, I will not be disgraced. Therefore, I have set my face like a stone, determined to do His will. And I know I will not be put to shame"* (Isaiah 50:7).

Of course, there will be obstacles and giants in the promised land of work who want to stop you, but you are well able to overcome them. The first battle is going to be against fear itself. Once that is won, the rest will be much easier.

SEE JOB SEEKER'S TIP #5: "Prepare for the Storm"

Your freedom from fear begins when you become convinced that God is good, that His love for you is perfect, and that He is all powerful. This is critical, because otherwise, you'll keep blaming Him for causing you harm or for looking away and leaving you on your own when trouble comes.

> *"Such love has no fear, because perfect love expels all fear. If we are afraid, it is for fear of punishment, and this shows that we have not fully experienced his perfect love"* (1 John 4:18).

If you're not sure about God's love for you, and about the power of that love to meet all your needs, start there. Ask God to reveal Himself to you. Find in His Word how Jesus demonstrated God's love for you. Become convinced that God is on your side and, as the apostle Paul stated, *"What shall we then say to these things? If God be for us, who can be against us?"* (Romans 8:31 KJV).

That's the foundation you need to stand on to put fear out of your life. More succinctly, get into right a relationship with God and you need fear nothing else.

Next, you need to be convinced that fear is not necessary. I once thought fear kept me motivated. Without fear and worry, I figured I'd just become a lazy slug. Nothing could be farther from the truth! Fear isn't a motivator; it paralyzes us and keeps us from achieving all that God has planned for us.

There are plenty of believers who think that fear is both necessary and helpful. When I dare job seekers to stop worrying, they push back. The typical response goes like this: "Well, of course, it would be nice if I didn't have to worry but that's not realistic. I'll stop worrying when I get to heaven. Until then I'll just have to live with it."

...You need to be convinced that fear is not necessary.

We're convinced that wrestling with anxiety is required of all adults. We aren't responsible grown-ups if we don't worry, right? Some of us even make fun of it, saying that we've elevated worrying to an art form. Unfortunately, this is no joke. How often do you really give your fears and anxieties to God? Most of us return time and again to fret about them, to remind God about them, and to spend a little more time trying to figure out how to handle them . . . just in case God doesn't feel like dealing with them. I hear this from job seekers all the time. They say they're trusting God for a new job, but just in case He doesn't come through in time, they're worrying about what they'll do for a backup plan.

If you're still not convinced about this whole "Fear Not" thing, consider this: if fear were necessary, God certainly would have given it to us. But He didn't and the Bible is crystal clear about that: *"For God has not given us a spirit of fear and timidity, but of power, love, and self-discipline"* (2 Timothy 1:7).

That's news to many of us. If God is not the author of fear, then it must be the product of a fallen world and a snare we don't need to step into, ever. To avoid the trap we'll start by identifying fear and all his relatives. It's important to recognize that worry, anxiety, panic and terror all fall under the general heading of fear. None of them come from God and Scripture tells us so.

- **Worry** — *"Then, turning to his disciples, Jesus said, 'That is why I tell you not to* ***worry*** *about everyday life — whether you have enough food to eat or enough clothes to wear. For life is more than food, and your body more than clothing. Look at the ravens. They don't plant or harvest or store food in barns, for God feeds them. And you are far more valuable to him than any birds! Can all your worries add a single moment to your life? And if worry can't accomplish a little thing like that, what's the use of worrying over bigger things?'"* (Luke 12:22-25).

- **Anxiety** — *"It is useless for you to work so hard from early morning until late at night,* ***anxiously*** *working for food to eat; for God gives rest to his loved ones"* (Psalm 127:2).

- **Fear** — *"We have been rescued from our enemies so we can serve God without* ***fear****"* (Luke 1:74) and *"****Fear*** *not, for I have redeemed you; I have called you by your name; You are Mine"* (Isaiah 43:1).

- **Terror** — *"Do not be* ***afraid*** *of the terrors of the night, nor the arrow that flies in the day"* (Psalm 91:5) *and "You will live in peace, and terror will not come near"* (Isaiah 54:14)

- **Panic** — *"But do not* ***panic****; don't be afraid when you hear the first rumor of approaching forces. For rumors will keep coming year by year"* (Jeremiah 51:46) and *"Hear, O Israel, today you are going into battle against your enemies. Do not be faintheart-*

> *ed or afraid; do not be terrified or give way to panic before them"* (Deuteronomy 20:3 NIV).

We could keep going because there are many scriptures just like these. I once counted nearly a hundred references to fear. What they all boil down to is simply this—Do not fear! Don't allow it, in any form, to enter into your thoughts. This is not a suggestion, it's a command. A little worry, a few moments of panic, and some anxious hours are all behaviors that believers simply cannot permit any longer.

Why is this such a big deal? When you allow fear into your heart, you surrender. It neutralizes you and renders you ineffective for Kingdom work. It will also seriously hamper your job search. Fear may well stop you from applying for a job if you've already decided you'll never get it. Fear can certainly prevent you from giving a good interview. And in failing to take these actions you may miss wonderful opportunities.

Job seekers all too often believe the self-defeating messages of a fallen world, accepting lies in place of the truth:

- "I'm afraid I'll never find a job that pays what I was making."
- "I'm worried that I'm too old to get hired."
- "What concerns me now is my lack of a college degree."

How can we reconcile doubts such as these with God's promise in Jeremiah 29:11? *"'For I know the plans I have for you,' declares the Lord, 'plans to prosper you and not to harm you, plans to give you hope and a future'"* (NIV).

We have tolerated fear and allowed it to contaminate our faith.

Our own words have made us sitting ducks and allowed the Enemy to steal our dreams, kill our opportunities and destroy our future. Now is the time to say, "No more and never again!" Just remember you are not alone. God will lend His strength and presence to help you whenever you feel yourself sinking into fear just as surely as Jesus reached out to catch Peter when his faith wavered and he began to sink.

So now we know that God doesn't use fear to accomplish His purposes, and He doesn't intend for us to allow it in our lives. But operating in this truth is easier said than done, isn't it? We've become so accustomed to entertaining fearful thoughts that it feels natural to us.

How many times have you said or thought, "Well, I'm only human. I can't help it if I get scared from time to time." The truth is that we can help it. God wouldn't have told us to "fear not" if this was impossible for us. Once again we find that we have a choice—this time the choice is to agree with fear . . . or not.

Whenever you speak the language of fear, you are surrendering to the world and putting yourself under its rule. When you speak with love and power, your Kingdom citizenship is obvious because your faith is in God and His word. It really is that simple. You do *not* have to be afraid, anxious, worried or panicked. You can choose to make fearlessness a reality in your life.

For many years, I thought fear was just a part of me, so I fought hard to manage my anxiety and control my fears. Instead of eliminating fear from my life I claimed it as mine and tried to work around it. Little did I know that the fear was not mine—I was under attack! I thought the presence of fear signaled that I had doubt and unbelief, that my faith was shaky. Now I know that those initial fearful thoughts just signaled that there was an enemy agent at the door. I have learned to keep the door shut. Perhaps you can't stop fearful thoughts from coming to call, but you sure don't have to invite them into your mind!

Do you doubt that you can live fearlessly? Do you still think that everyone has to experience anxiety when facing difficult situations like a job loss? If so, allow me to present a scenario for you.

Perhaps you can't stop fearful thoughts from coming to call, but you sure don't have to invite them into your mind!

Imagine that you've had cancer for a number of years and that just recently the doctors discovered it is no longer in remission. Not only that, but the disease has damaged your liver so badly that only a transplant can save you. So you're on the waiting list for a new one, but no one knows when a donor might be found. In this same time frame, your spouse has just suffered both a stroke and a heart attack that has left him blind and very weak. The final blow comes when your employer announces that your job has been eliminated. You are the sole support for your household and within a few weeks all of your medical benefits will end along with your paycheck. Is it possible to be fearless in the midst of all that? I know it is, because I've personally witnessed it.

That was the actual story of a beautiful woman named Jean who had been assigned to me for outplacement counseling. I quickly learned that she was a believer who knew there was absolutely no way she could handle all that she was facing on her own. So together we took the entire situation to the Lord and left it at His feet. At the end of our session, Jean made this statement: "There is nothing I can do about any of this but I will not fear. This is way too big for me so I'm leaving it with the Lord. I will trust Him and I will stay in peace. Now I'm going to go home and spend time with my husband and wait to see what the Lord will do."

Jean certainly sounded like she meant what she said. I never saw her again but I did get a call from her three months later. Naturally, I asked how she was doing and this is what she told me. "I went home and did just what I said I was going to do. My husband and I puttered around fixing the house, reading the Word, and praising God. We had a wonderful time together. I continued to sing in my church choir and volunteered for little projects. During this time God healed both my husband and me. My white blood cell count is now normal and the doctors can find no sign of cancer. I'm even off the waiting list for a donor because my liver is healing and I no longer need it.

"My husband is stronger and able to see again. He walks up to the church a few times a week and serves as an associate pastor part-time, something he has always wanted to do. Not only that, but the company just called and offered me my old job back with a better title and a much higher salary. Apparently they discovered that my position was critical, and I have the skills they need. So I had a wonderful break from work and now God has restored everything to me. I never lost one night of sleep, and I never spent one moment worrying. It was the greatest experience of my life!"

Now, obviously, it was God's will to handle Jean's health situation in this way, and even to restore her job. Certainly, that will not always be the case. Let me make this perfectly clear: Faithful, godly believers die of diseases every day, so being sick certainly is not a sign that you lack faith or that you missed God. We will never understand all the mysteries of this life or why things work out as they do. Just know that God loves you and He has a good plan for your life, both now and eternally.[8] Whatever it is that is keeping you up at night is simply a belief that God can't fix it, that He doesn't care, or that His way isn't always the best for you. Those are the lies that will cripple you. It was this woman's experience that proved to me that God means it when He says "Fear not" and that we have the ability to follow that direction.

That brings us to the how-to part of the process. The best illustration I've ever found for eliminating fear comes from Jesus. In Luke 8:49 we read the story of Jairus, whose daughter was near death when he found Jesus and asked him to come heal her. You might recall that Jesus was delayed by the woman who touched his garment and was healed. As he was about to continue, *"someone came from the ruler of the synagogue's house, saying to him, 'Your daughter is dead. Do not trouble the Teacher.' But when Jesus heard it, He answered him, saying, 'Do not be afraid; only believe, and she will be made well'"* (Luke 8:49-50 NKJV).

Belief in God's love and goodness toward you will help to overcome fear. What are you fretting about right now? Go into His Word and find out what He has to say about your need. If you're plagued by the thought that your money is running out, remember that Philippians 4:19 tells us:

"And this same God who takes care of me will supply all your needs from his glorious riches, which have been given to us in Christ Jesus." Your needs will be covered. If God promised it, you can take it to the bank!

At the same time, you must continue to do your part to provide income, whether that means taking a part-time job, having a yard sale, or some other means of earning income until your job situa-

8. See Jeremiah 29:11

tion improves. God will lead you and provide you with all the ideas that you need. Just don't forget that you are responsible for acting; He is responsible for the results.

Read all the promises of God's provisions and build your confidence in His Word. Then, when fear comes knocking, stand your ground!

Fear works best where there is no Word and no personal relationship with God. We cannot stand on promises we don't know and we can't overcome our enemy without God giving us the strategy.

We'll spend time later learning about all we have inherited in Christ and how to confront the challenges we face. But for right now, you can jump-start your fearless living by remembering that if a thought brings fear, God's Word contains the remedy. James 4:7 says *"Therefore submit to God. Resist the devil and he will flee from you"* (NKJV). Submit to God by putting all your confidence in what He has promised. Resist the devil by praising God and thanking Him for the overcoming work of Jesus Christ. If you start to waver, return to Colossians 2:15 and remind yourself that Jesus has completely destroyed the works of the Enemy so you have no reason to be afraid of him anymore.

SEE JOB SEEKER'S TIP #6: *"Facing Your Giants"*

Just as God has specific turnaround strategies for job seekers, our Adversary has specific shut-down strategies that he uses against believers. His methods are so subtle that job seekers often fall for them without even knowing they're being snared. Every one of his tactics is designed to accomplish the same goal—to get you to sit down and quit. You must keep moving if you want God to lead you to victory. After all, He cannot steer an anchored ship, can He?

I've observed across the years what I believe are the Enemy's favorite three-part strategies to render you helpless:

- Offense, Anger and Revenge
- Guilt, Shame and Condemnation
- Confusion, Distraction and Procrastination

Each of these strategies starts with an attempt to isolate the job seeker. The effectiveness of these tactics will decrease dramatically if you stay connected to others. "*A person standing alone can be attacked and defeated, but two can stand back-to-back and conquer. Three are even better, for a triple-braided cord is not easily broken*" (Ecclesiastes 4:12).

Go to church, volunteer, and stay connected to family and friends.

I'll admit that it's tough to get out and socialize with others when you're out of work. People always ask about the job search and frequently offer unhelpful, even painful, feedback and advice. We'll spend more time on this later, but for now, just take my word for it and stay in the Body. Go to church, volunteer, and stay connected to family and friends. This is one time when there really is safety in numbers.

Let's look at the first trap—Offense, Anger and Revenge. This is a very effective method of keeping job seekers stuck in the past. It works particularly well in situations where an employer did something illegal or blatantly unjustified. Anyone who has experienced discrimination or who was forced out of a position without cause is likely to be susceptible to the suggestion to sue that former employer and get revenge for the wrongdoing. What a trap this is! I've seen job seekers spend all their money and energy on lawyers, going after a former employer, only to end up months later with absolutely nothing.

This doesn't mean there aren't legitimate reasons to take legal action against a former employer, but for the believer, revenge is never one of them. God has cautioned us about this. *"I will take revenge; I will pay them back. In due time, their feet will slip. Their day of disaster will arrive, and their destiny will overtake them"* (Deuteronomy 32:35).

That makes His position on the matter pretty clear, doesn't it? No matter what happened to you, do not act out of revenge. Instead, turn your focus to the future and let the Lord get you situated in a new position. Then, if He wants you to be a whistle blower, expose wrongdoing, or whatever, you'll be able to do so without anger or revenge in mind.

No matter what happened to you, do not act out of revenge.

The second strategy is the Enemy's quit-early-and-avoid-the-rush tactic. With this one he brings up the past to see if he can ensnare you with Guilt, Shame and Condemnation before you even start your job search. It's a great strategy to use with job seekers who already feel responsible for losing their jobs.

Years ago there was a famous cartoon in which the lead character declared "We have met the enemy and he is us!" This epitomizes the job seeker who buys into self-condemnation and gives up in hopelessness even before getting started.

Here's why you don't need to fall into this trap either. There is nothing you have done, or could ever do, that is bigger than the redemption of Christ Jesus. He is sitting at the right hand of God right now, interceding on your behalf. What He has done for you is more than enough to compensate for anything you've ever messed up.

Remember, too, that your present situation is not a surprise to God. He has already seen the end of your life on this planet and He has a plan to bring you through in triumph. If you're still alive then there's something more God has for you to accomplish! Never fall for the lie that you don't deserve a good job or that you've committed the unpardonable work mistake. Instead, turn your focus back on God and follow the advice in Isaiah 43:18-19: *"Forget the former things; do not dwell on the past. See, I am doing a new thing! Now it springs up; do you not perceive it? I am making a way in the desert and streams in the wasteland"* (NIV).

Now that's a great deal! You give God your past, with all its wastelands, and He'll make a way out of the desert for you! I saw this in action a few years ago. One of the job seekers in my small group had been working in a prison as a deputy. Jim felt that he had been called by God to be a light in the prison system and that he blew it. Apparently he placed too much trust in an inmate and had been fired for causing a security breach.

When Jim showed up in our group that first night he was convinced that he had failed and that he would never be able to achieve the destiny God had for Him. Then he heard that message in Isaiah 43 and he realized that God had called him to this field knowing full well that he would make this mistake. That's when everything turned around for him. Within a week he had called another prison and arranged an interview. He was completely open about what he had done and what he had learned. And he was hired on the spot. Get this—his new boss said that his mistake was the reason he got the job! It was obvious that he would never make a security mistake like that again, and his honesty about the situation had proved his trustworthiness!

That brings us to the third snare, and this is the sneakiest one of all. I believe this one captures more job seekers than the first two combined. When Confusion, Distraction and Procrastination come into play, job seekers drop out of the hunt and don't even realize they've been trapped.

If you're unemployed right now, you may have already found yourself wandering around the house wondering what to do next. Maybe you went online to find some companies with open positions. After a little while, you were distracted by a news story, your homepage, YouTube videos, or someone at the door. Soon after, you felt hungry, so you wandered off to find something to eat. Then you noticed that the refrigerator was dirty so you emptied it out and cleaned it. The next thing you knew, the day was half over and you'd made no progress at all on your job search. To keep from becoming depressed, you turned on the television and vowed to try again tomorrow. When this string of events repeats often enough, depression will set in and you'll be out of the running.

If this sounds familiar, don't despair. As always, God has provided a release from this trap. "*With the Lord's authority I say this: Live no longer as the Gentiles* [unbelievers] *do, for they are hopelessly confused. Their minds are full of darkness; they wander far from the life God gives because they have closed their minds and hardened their hearts against Him*" (Ephesians 4:17).

God has a perfect and well-ordered plan for your life and work but you have to spend time with Him if you want Him to direct your path. That's why the project planning process is so important. Job seekers can't afford to wake up in the morning without a clear set of marching orders for the day. So before we even get started on mastering the job search process and getting prepared to enter the marketplace, we should take some time to establish a daily routine and commit to the discipline to follow it.

One key piece of advice here: unplug your TV during the day! Also, make sure that everything you do online directly relates to your job search. Set a limit on the time you spend on the Internet. Whether you realize it or not, both the television and the computer are powerful distractions from the Word of God and can cause you to wander far from the path He has prepared for you.

You can sidestep all three of these traps by looking forward, not to the past, and by joining the apostle Paul, who realized how to completely break free. *"I have not achieved it, but I focus on this one thing: Forgetting the past and looking forward to what lies ahead, I press on to reach the end of the race and receive the heavenly prize for which God, through Christ Jesus, is calling us"* (Philippians 3:13-14). That's the real bottom line, keeping our focus on Jesus and our eternal promise. Every time we allow our focus to turn to self—our past, our actions, our plans, our self interests—we open ourselves to fear. As long as we stay rooted and grounded in Christ we will experience the promise of Isaiah 26:3: *"You will keep him in perfect peace, Whose mind is stayed on You, Because he trusts in You"* (NKJV).

It's not the ultimate goal to simply defend yourself either. You need to pick up the spiritual weapons you've been given and take back the workplace for the glory of God. As you might guess, we'll start with the spiritual armor that has been provided for our protection. So suit up before you go out.

> *"Put on the full armor of God so that you can take your stand against the devil's schemes. For our struggle is not against flesh and blood, but against the rulers, against the authorities, against the powers of this dark world and against the spiritual forces of evil in the heavenly realms. Therefore put on the full armor of God, so that when the day of evil comes, you may be able to stand your ground, and after you have done everything, to stand. Stand firm then, with the belt of truth buckled around your waist, with the breastplate of righteousness in place, and with your feet fitted with the readiness that comes from the gospel of peace. In addition to all this, take up the shield of faith, with which you can extinguish all the flaming arrows of the evil one. Take the helmet of salvation and the sword of the Spirit, which is the word of God"* (Ephesians 6:11-17 NIV).

I once thought this was just a neat word picture. Now I understand that it comes directly from our "owner's manual" and we'd be wise to do exactly what it tells us. We need to cover our heads and fill our minds with all of the salvation messages in the Word.

We need to cover our heads and fill our minds with all of the salvation messages in the Word.

You have been saved unto eternal life and you have received some blessings that will make a tremendous difference in this life as well. That's important to know. You can rely on the truth of God to give you real confidence as you approach the marketplace. The righteousness that is yours because of Jesus will be your spiritual protection against everything the world can throw at you—and it will throw everything at you. His peace will secure you against the storms that are sure to come. And faith, the ability to wait expectantly on the promises you receive from God, is your fuel for the entire job search process.

Finally, the sword of the Spirit, which is the Word of God, is the weapon that causes the Enemy to flee before you. You will need this armor if you're going to fight the battle without getting wounded. So as the saying goes, "don't leave home without it!"

In addition to protective armor, you have been given other wonderful weapons. We have already seen that God's Word is a mighty sword that cuts through the darkness and renders every worldly attack harmless. If you're worried that you don't know enough Bible verses, you'll appreciate the next weapon because it's available to even a brand new believer.

This weapon, one of my personal favorites, is Praise. Take a look at 2 Chronicles 20:20-24 and you'll see how well praise works. In this story enemy forces had gathered to attack the people of God. However, His people took up the weapon of praise:

> *"At the very moment they began to sing and give praise, the Lord caused the armies of Ammon, Moab, and Mount Seir to start fighting among themselves. The armies of Moab and Ammon turned against their allies from Mount Seir and killed every one of them. After they had destroyed the army of Seir, they began attacking each other. So when the army of Judah arrived at the lookout point in the wilderness, all they saw were dead bodies lying on the ground as far as they could see. Not a single one of the enemy had escaped."*

I strongly suggest you try this. Lead off with praise in the morning, walk in obedience and love throughout the day and see if you don't end the day with a sense of personal victory. This is one powerful strategy for overcoming the depression that often plagues job seekers.

Prayer is yet another awesome weapon. It's so critical to your job search success that we'll be spending a lot of time on it. If you doubt the power of prayer, consider this passage:

"*But while Peter was in prison, the church prayed very earnestly for him. The night before Peter was to be placed on trial, he was asleep, fastened with two chains between two soldiers. Others stood guard at the prison gate. Suddenly, there was a bright light in the cell, and an angel of the Lord stood before Peter. The angel struck him on the side to awaken him and said, 'Quick! Get up!' And the chains fell off his wrists. Then the angel told him, 'Get dressed and put on your sandals.' And he did. 'Now put on your coat and follow me,' the angel ordered. So Peter left the cell, following the angel. But all the time he thought it was a vision. He didn't realize it was actually happening. They passed the first and second guard posts and came to the iron gate leading to the city, and this opened for them all by itself. So they passed through and started walking down the street, and then the angel suddenly left him*" (Acts 12:5-9). This happened so quickly and was so amazing that Peter thought he was dreaming. It wasn't until he found himself alone on the street that it occurred to him that he had actually been set free!

Scripture also tells us of another powerful weapon in God's arsenal—an entire army of angels.[9] Once again I find that I must clarify what I mean here because of the mania going on about angels in the New Age movement and elsewhere. I am not saying that every good thing that happens to us is the work of heavenly hosts. They are not supernatural fairy godmothers. Nor are they to be prayed to or worshiped as so many now do. Once again the world system

9. See Hebrews 1:14

has attempted to pervert a gift from God to His people. Just know this, angels really are a weapon God has provided to minister to us and to fight on our behalf at His command and they are a formidable force. I love the story in 2 Kings 6:16-17 when the prophet and his servant appeared to be completely outnumbered. That poor servant was sure they were doomed. *"'Don't be afraid,' the prophet answered. 'Those who are with us are more than those who are with them.' And Elisha prayed, 'O Lord, open his eyes so he may see.' Then the Lord opened the servant's eyes, and he looked and saw the hills full of horses and chariots of fire all around Elisha"* (NIV). God still charges His angels to *"keep you in all your ways"* (Psalm 91:11 NKJV).

This isn't the complete list of weapons in your arsenal by any means, but it gives you an idea of the firepower on our side. Let's recap where our discussion has led us so far. Hopefully we are agreed that God is not in the fear business, and that He has directed us to adopt a zero tolerance policy toward every form of fear in our lives. Fear will continue to show up on your doorstep from time to time, but that doesn't obligate you to invite it in as your houseguest. Once fear is sent packing, it becomes possible to see and think more clearly.

It should also be apparent by now that there is much more at stake here than your next work assignment. God is using this season of unemployment or employment transition to train and equip you to be more than a conqueror. I used to wonder what that phrase meant. After all, conquerors win every battle, every time. What could be better or greater than that? Then I realized that God is offering us a battle plan that ensures our victory and showers us with blessings as we fight! What would you call a season of testing and training that makes us complete and lacking nothing by the time we finish it? That's His plan and it's just like our heavenly Father to provide it for His children.

But after discovering all this, one other thing becomes clear—there's far more to your Kingdom citizenship than you might have imagined. If you just keep pursuing the Kingdom, God will reveal everything you've been given as a joint heir with Christ Jesus. As you learn more about this awesome plan of God, I hope you're getting excited about the possibilities that lie ahead of you. I also hope that, from this point forward, the phrase "fear of the Lord" will only cause you to pause in wonder and marvel at a Father who loves you this perfectly; a King who has done wonderful things to ensure your victory. From this moment on, that's the only fear you'll ever need in your life!

CHAPTER THREE

1. What does God say about fear in the life of a believer?

2. What is the harm of a little worry or fear? Isn't it only natural?

3. How do we eliminate fear from our lives?

4. What strategies do job seekers need to guard against? Have you seen evidence of this? Where?

5. What comprises the full armor of God?

6. What other weapons are at your disposal?

JOB SEEKER'S TIP #5 Prepare for the Storm

I live in Florida. At least once a year everyone here goes through the drill of preparing for an oncoming hurricane. We buy flashlight batteries, bottled water, and nonperishable food supplies. We secure all our lawn furniture and let water out of our pools in preparation for a possible deluge. When I do this, I'm not motivated by fear or panic. I just want to ensure that my family won't be unduly inconvenienced by the effects of a storm. Job seekers need to take proactive action to minimize the damage of sudden unemployment as well as to bring assurance to their families by behaving with calm, faith-based confidence.

Storms will happen. We shouldn't expect to escape all the trials of life. God's Word tells us that we will have to walk through difficult situations. But James 1:2-4 tells us that there is a great benefit to the trials we face: *"Consider it pure joy, my brothers, whenever you face trials of many kinds, because you know that the testing of your faith develops perseverance. Perseverance must finish its work so that you may be mature and complete, not lacking anything"* (NIV). Every significant challenge we face gives us another opportunity to grow deep roots of faith and become more and more unshakable.

When you find yourself out of work, don't hide your head in the sand and hope everything will be okay. Assess your situation and take action.

Make sure you're tithing and giving. This instruction from God is for our benefit and it is your way of demonstrating that you belong to

His Kingdom. *"'Bring the whole tithe into the storehouse, that there may be food in my house. Test me in this,' says the Lord Almighty, 'and see if I will not throw open the floodgates of heaven and pour out so much blessing that there will not be room enough for it'"* (Malachi 3:10 NIV). (Give your time if you have no money.)

- ***File for unemployment immediately.***
- ***Sign up for children's health insurance coverage through your state, if available.***
- ***Do your research. Identify potential sources of financial support. What church resources, agencies, and emergency funding might be available to you? Complete all the applications for support before you need it.***
- ***Contact all relatives and close friends to let them know what has happened. See who might be willing and able to lend support.***
- ***Write to all creditors immediately. Explain your situation, state your commitment to pay your debts, and ask for arrangements to postpone or reduce your payments temporarily.***
- ***Consolidate all your consumer loans. Defer any payments if possible. Make all possible cash flow reductions.***
- ***Engage everyone in cost-cutting measures. Get your family involved in the storm preparation.***
- ***Seek income-producing opportunities. What can you sell? What can you barter? What can you make or do to generate income? Get creative.***
- ***Keep God at the center of all your decisions and DO NOT FEAR!***

JOB SEEKER'S TIP #6 Facing Your Giants

Is there something in your past that has you worried? Are you concerned that this one thing might keep you from getting a new job, a better job, or maybe any job at all? Don't duck the issue or hope it will never come up. Chances are, if it's bothering you it will come up in every interview until you deal with it! Don't let it cripple you or limit your plans for the future by bringing up things in the past. God has already made a way out for you.

This is the perfect time to deal with your issue. Repent, if you need to, and receive God's forgiveness. Then do as God does and forget it. Paul said it best, *"But one thing I do: forgetting what is behind and straining toward what is ahead, I press on toward the goal to win the prize for which God has called me heavenward in Christ Jesus"* (Philippians 3:13-14 NIV). There's nothing in your past that you and Jesus can't handle together.

One or more of the following tactics will help you to be victorious in every case.

- ***Get help.*** If you don't know how to write a résumé, find someone who does. If you don't know who could use your skills, ask professionals in the field you are seeking to give you feedback. Find someone to help you with any obstacle you can't handle on your own.

- ***Renew your mind.*** You might be holding on to an irrational or outdated belief. Example: It's easier to find a job when you already have a job. If your belief is hurting you, drop it. Change your mind on negative, self-defeating thoughts. Find out what the Word has to say about you and stand on it!

- ***Make changes.*** Is your answering machine message silly? Does your e-mail address, personal website, Facebook or LinkedIn page say something about you that you'd rather not advertise to prospective employers? Change them! Do your clothes make you look unprofessional? Change them! Don't know how to talk to strangers? Learn!

- ***Find the right place to look.*** If you love having spiky, blue hair or you refuse to give up your denim jeans, find places to work that feel the same as you do on those issues. Don't waste your time trying to get into places where the workers are held to a different standard. The only person who will love and accept you unconditionally and just as you are on this planet is your mother (and that's only if you're very fortunate!)

- ***Have a good answer.*** This is usually your very best solution. Face the thing you're most afraid of head on. What happened? Why did it happen? Now, what did you learn? How have you changed? What assurance can you offer that it won't happen again? Who will verify that the problem wasn't you? When you think you have a good answer, go and tell it to a trusted, objective professional and ask for candid feedback. Keep working until you can give your answer without undue emotion and without creating concern in the listener.

Sure, there may be giants to face before you can possess the blessing God has for you and the work you desire, but with the help of the Holy Spirit, you are well able to overcome them!

CHAPTER 4

CHOOSE

"You didn't choose me. I chose you. I appointed you to go and produce lasting fruit, so that the Father will give you whatever you ask for, using my name."

– John 15:16

"Choose for yourselves this day whom you will serve. . . . But as for me and my household, we will serve the Lord."

– Joshua 24:15 (NIV)

If ever there was a passage of Scripture designed especially with job seekers in mind, Matthew 6:31-33 would have to be it. *"So do not worry, saying, 'What shall we eat?' or 'What shall we drink?' or 'What shall we wear?' For the pagans run after all these things, and your heavenly Father knows that you need them. But seek first his kingdom and his righteousness, and all these things will be given to you as well"* (NIV).

We seek the Kingdom of God and His will, and everything we need is given to us. Note the word is "need," not "want." This seems pretty clear, and there's strong evidence that life in God's economy works. After the disciples had traveled a while with Jesus, He sent them out in pairs to carry on the work of the Gospel. Just like many job seekers, they went out without income, savings accounts, or supplies. Later Jesus asked them about their experience with a Kingdom support plan. And He said to them, *"'When I sent you without money bag, knapsack, and sandals, did you lack anything?' So they said, 'Nothing'"* (Luke 22:35 NKJV).

When this Scripture first caught my attention, I was in need of everything. My own method of meeting my needs wasn't working, so I decided I would give this Kingdom-seeking business a serious try. If there was some other way to live and to take care of my family, I wanted to know about it. Could this describe you, too? Has your job loss motivated you to find out how God really intends for you to live?

Maybe your heart is telling you, as mine did, that there has to be a better way. I hope so, because I found that openness and desire will put you in the perfect position to receive all the blessings God wants to give in this transition season. We've already talked about how God can transform an employment crisis into a blessing, and how believers can triumph over fear in the midst of this experience. Now you can discover how to turn your job search into a Kingdom search as well, and how to experience the life of an "overcomer."

Then again, maybe you're not interested in seeking the Kingdom right now. Perhaps, because you have your hands full just trying to find a job or keep one, you don't think this is the time to take on another new project. You're not alone. It's not uncommon for job seekers to show up in our small group planning only to get job leads or help with their resumes. When it becomes obvious that our group is first and foremost a Bible study and only secondarily a job seeker's support group, some choose not to stay. Frequently they'll say, "I appreciate the importance of Bible study but I need to focus all my attention on my job search right now. I have real-life needs and just don't have time for this spiritual stuff. Maybe I'll come back once I land my next job and things settle down."

Many of these folks have already conducted job searches and been successful on their own. They figure they'll just do what they did before and all will be well. Unfortunately, that's not always the case. More than a few have come back to the group weeks or months later, and because the old approach failed to deliver the expected results, they're ready to try it God's way.

Please don't misunderstand what I'm saying here. They did not fail because God did something to them. When God tells us to seek His Kingdom and His righteousness it is not because it makes Him feel good to get our attention. He's trying to protect us and bless us. Those job seekers were unsuccessful because they, like so many other believers, didn't understand or refused to believe that we are in the middle of a war between two kingdoms and the conflict is heating up. As I said earlier, it doesn't matter if you don't want to be on the battlefield. That's where you are. And, it doesn't matter if you just want to do things the old way to get the same old results. That's no longer an option. To understand why the old way no longer works for you, let's look at what happened the day you were born again.

...It doesn't matter if you don't want to be on the battlefield. That's where you are.

"May you be filled with joy, always thanking the Father. He has enabled you to share in the inheritance that belongs to his people, who live in the light. For he has rescued us

> *from the kingdom of darkness and transferred us into the Kingdom of his dear Son, who purchased our freedom and forgave our sins"* (Colossians 1:11-14).
>
> *"Even before He made the world, God loved us and chose us in Christ to be holy and without fault in his eyes"* (Ephesians 1:4).

God selected you. Through Christ, you were redeemed, made blameless and welcomed into His Kingdom. But God didn't just give you new citizenship and a place in His family. He also gave each one of us a Kingdom assignment. *"You didn't choose me. I chose you. I appointed you to go and produce lasting fruit, so that the Father will give you whatever you ask for, using my name"* (John 15:16).

You have been chosen for a very specific purpose—to produce lasting fruit for God's Kingdom! To make that possible He also arranged for everything that you would require to ensure your success.

You have been given authority over all things. *"What are mere mortals that you should think about them, or a son of man that you should care for him? Yet you made them only a little lower than the angels and crowned them with glory and honor. You gave them authority over all things"* (Hebrews 2:6-8).

"All things" means nothing is left out. But we have not yet seen all things put under our authority. What we do see is Jesus, the perfect Man. And because He suffered death for us, He is now "crowned with glory and honor." *"God, for whom and through whom everything was made, chose to bring many children into glory. And it was only right that he should make Jesus, through his suffering, a perfect leader, fit to bring them into their salvation"* (Hebrews 2:10).

Let's look a little closer. Jesus came to destroy the works of the Enemy and to take back dominion over this world. He accomplished His mission. Now He is positioned at the right hand of God as our Perfect Leader.

We're now being trained to assume our Kingdom assignments and to walk in the power and authority He has given us in Christ. We may not have realized it, but everything changed the day we accepted Christ. We all know that we were forgiven and we received eternal life when we were born again. What many of us didn't realize was that, at that same moment, the very power that raised Jesus from the dead came to reside as the Spirit of God in us! This is what Paul tells us in Ephesians 1:19:

> *"I also pray that you will understand the incredible greatness of God's power for us who believe him. This is the same mighty power that raised Christ from the dead and seated him in the place of honor at God's right hand in the heavenly realms. Now he is far above any ruler or authority or power or leader or anything else—not only in this world but also in the world to come. God has put all things under the authority of Christ and has made him head over all things for the benefit of the church. And the church is his body; it is made full and complete by Christ, who fills all things everywhere with himself."*

Like treasure hidden in earthen vessels, we have the very spirit of God living within us![10] Do you understand? Christ is the head and we are now His body. We have been equipped to do great things in the name of Christ who has filled us with Himself!

Consider what that means to you as a job seeker. No matter what you've done, no matter how many mistakes you've made at work

10. See 2 Corinthians 4:6-7 KJV

or in life, God has determined that you are forgiven, effective immediately, if you will receive the gift of Jesus Christ as your Lord and Savior. You and I will never need to accept defeat of any sort in our job searches or lives ever again. Through obedience to God we can pursue our eternal destiny for the pleasure and glory of God!

The moment we accept Jesus as Lord, our spirits come alive and God starts working in us to make us like Jesus.

You might be reacting like I did when I first heard this bit of news. My response was, "I don't think so." It was pretty obvious to me that I was defeated. In fact, most days I very much looked and felt like I had been on the losing side of a long, hard battle. But I now realize that we really are transformed at the new birth. The moment we accept Jesus as Lord, our spirits come alive and God starts working in us to make us like Jesus.

> *"Dear friends, we are already God's children, but he has not yet shown us what we will be like when Christ appears. But we do know that we will be like him, for we will see him as he really is"* (1 John 3:2).

Now let's go back to those believers who don't want to seek the Kingdom right now, who want to put it off until they have time for it. You can probably see why that's not a wise decision. You may not have realized what happened when you were saved, but the Enemy certainly did. He knows that the Spirit of God now dwells in you and he's afraid you might learn to listen to that voice and follow it. He knows that God didn't just adopt you—He also *hired* you for His Kingdom purposes and that makes you dangerous.

Now you know what God had in mind when He chose you; He intended you to have power and authority to complete the mission He's given you. If that doesn't motivate you for your job search, then perhaps this next revelation will. It's what you agreed to when you accepted God's offer of salvation.

Think back to the day you were saved. What did you say when you accepted Christ? Maybe it was something like "Jesus, forgive my sins. I give you my life." Or "Jesus, I believe that you died for me. I make you my Lord and Savior." Whatever words you uttered, here's the deal you made: You gave Jesus your old life, and you accepted the new life He died to give you. It was not a one-way thing, it was an exchange. When you made Jesus your Lord, you relinquished all rights to yourself.

> *"Do you not know that your body is a temple of the Holy Spirit, who is in you, whom you have received from God? You are not your own; you were bought at a price"* (1 Corinthians 6:19-20 NIV).

Most of us, having been raised under democratic forms of government, don't really understand what it's like to have a King, Lord or Master. Consequently, on the day we were reborn, we may not have understood that we enlisted for life and put on a Kingdom uniform. It was also the day we agreed to abide by all His laws and commands. We agreed to be ruled by God with Jesus as our Lord and Master.

So you see, we don't really have the right to choose how we proceed at this point. We gave ourselves to God and now belong to Him. He desires to change us into the image of Christ. He wants to demonstrate His love and His power through us. And we owe Him our obedience. If we're going to have a successful tour of duty, we will need to learn the rules of our new Kingdom. After all, that's what we signed up for when we accepted Jesus as our Lord and Savior. More than that, our obedience is the way we can show Jesus our love for all He has done for us.

It's sad, but after being adopted into God's Kingdom and family, believers often drag their feet and delay their blessings in this new way of life. Many enter the Kingdom of God but never really allow God to change them. They behave as immigrants who come to a new country but maintain their original customs and lifestyles. No doubt you've seen these communities. You turn a corner and suddenly all the storefront signs are in another language. The people living there seldom venture far from that neighborhood, and they never receive all the benefits of their new country. They are free to come and go but they live as if they're held captive. In fact, they are prisoners of their past.

Unfortunately, so are many believers. They don't even know that they're living a restricted life until something happens to rock their world. Then they discover they have been victimized and feel powerless. That's when many believers cry out to God for His help. As I said before, the good news is that God can take a horrible work experience or a job loss and use it to lead a believer straight to the power, authority and guaranteed victory in Christ.

So where do you stand? Do you have the courage to change your top priority from a quest for a new job to a quest for a new Kingdom? I'm sure fear will tell you that if you take your eyes off your job search you'll starve, or go under and take your whole family with you. That's not the way God operates, I assure you. In Matthew, chapters 14 and 16, we see that Jesus knew when people were hungry and He fed them, using the power of God in a miraculous way. A good shepherd sees to it that his sheep are fed and protected.

> *"Which of you, if his son asks for bread, will give him a stone? Or if he asks for a fish, will give him a snake? If you, then, though you are evil, know how to give good gifts to your children, how much more will your Father in heaven give good gifts to those who ask him!"* (Matthew 7:9-11 NIV).

Our loving God has the ultimate say in our lives. No matter what may come our way, trusting Him with *every* part of our lives—including our job search—is the safest and wisest thing we can do.

God is well aware of your situation.

Let me say this one more time: God is well aware of your situation. It's no surprise to Him that you are currently out of work or perhaps in a job that brings you no joy. Not only is He aware of your circumstance, He wants to use it to show you how to act upon His promises in your life. His offer remains: *"So don't worry about these things, saying, 'What will we eat? What will we drink? What will we wear?' These things dominate the thoughts of unbelievers, but your heavenly Father already knows all your needs. Seek the Kingdom of God above all else, and live righteously, and he will give you everything you need"* (Matthew 6:31-33).

Will you trust Him to come through on this promise? Now is a great time to say "Yes." You need a victory in your job search or transition and God really wants you to have it. Your victory will bring Him glory. Your outstanding success through the entire process is precisely what will get the Kingdom of God the attention He is after.

This dark and hurting world needs to see believers demonstrate the overcoming life God offers. *"You are the light of the world. A city that is set on a hill cannot be hidden"* (Matthew 5:14 NKJV). So you have nothing to lose and everything to gain if you choose to do your job search God's way.

Believe me, the job search process alone is tough enough. When believers have to contend with the Enemy's attacks as well, it's time to call in heavenly reinforcements! So say "Yes!" to what God is offering for the battle—His royal backing and all the resources of His heavenly Kingdom. You're already wearing a Kingdom uniform. All that's left now is to get the understanding and training you need to demonstrate His Sovereign power to the rest of the world!

Oh, and in case you were wondering, there really is no third option. As I stated in the beginning, it's God's way or the world's way. There is no neutral territory, no demilitarized zone, and no negotiating a truce with the world. Trying to live in submission to the laws of both kingdoms is like trying to maintain balance while standing in two canoes. It can't be done. *"No one can serve two masters. For you will hate one and love the other; you will be devoted to one and despise the other"* (Matthew 6:24).

My hope is that you have decided to put both feet in God's canoe and tackle your job search using the resources of the Kingdom. Let me be the first to welcome you to your Kingdom Orientation program. To help get you started I've identified the questions you might be asking about your new job—the one God is offering you.

What's my title and who will I report to?

You've been hired to fill a Disciple position, working directly for Jesus. This is an entry-level position that leads to an assignment as Ambassador for Christ, and God will be personally involved in your training. He will be joined in this effort by the Holy Spirit who will serve as your Guide and Teacher throughout the duration of your employment on earth. Should the going get difficult, the Holy Spirit is also fully prepared to provide comfort and support as needed.

What will I be doing?

You will be learning how to conduct an excellent job search while completing the small project assignments God gives you during your time out of the workplace. As soon as you're prepared, you'll be out looking for a job and practicing the laws of the Kingdom system—love, forgiveness, faith and gratitude—in real-life situations. You will be expected to keep moving and acting on the instructions you're given. Then the Holy Spirit will be able to add the super power of God to your natural best and produce supernatural success. The great news is that you no longer need to worry about finding a new job! In fact, as we discovered earlier, He is expecting you to give up every form of fear, including worry, so that you will be able to clearly hear His instructions. Be advised, though, this is a very challenging program. It will take all your energy and time to complete it, but you will never be left to figure things out on your own. Everything you need to know has been written down in His Word, so the more you study it the faster you'll progress.

How am I expected to perform?

God's biggest expectation is that you will take Him at His word and accept His commands and His promises by faith. It takes real effort to misunderstand this: *"And it is impossible to please God without faith . . ."* (Hebrews 11:6). That means you'll be doing some things that won't make any sense to your natural mind. Your best course will be to immediately act on whatever you're told. Your action plan can be summed up as follows: *"Don't copy the behavior and customs of this world, but let God transform you into a new person by changing the way you think. Then you will learn to know God's will for you, which is good and pleasing and perfect"* (Romans 12:2).

SEE JOB SEEKER'S TIP #7: } *"What Job Are You Looking For?"*

Make no mistake—you have not accepted an easy job. G.K. Chesterton had it right when he said, *"Christianity has not been tried and found wanting; it has been found difficult and not tried."* Jesus Himself understood how difficult it would be to switch kingdoms and follow Him by faith. He said, *"But don't begin until you count the cost. For who would begin construction of a building without first calculating the cost to see if there is enough money to finish it? Otherwise, you might complete only the foundation before running out of money, and then everyone would laugh at you. They would say, 'There's the person who started that building and couldn't afford to finish it!' Or what king would go to war against another king without first sitting down with his counselors to discuss whether his army of 10,000 could defeat the 20,000 soldiers marching against him? And if he can't, he will send a delegation to discuss terms of peace while the enemy is still far away. So you cannot become my disciple without giving up everything you own"* (Luke 14:28-33).

This position will also require that you check with God about every decision you make and every action you take. The closer you get to Him and the more time you spend learning how He wants things done, the better you will be at your job.

How will I be trained for this assignment?

There will be three key phases to your Kingdom job search process—Ask, Seek and Knock. Each phase has been designed to increase your awareness of the laws of the Kingdom and to build your skill in using the power and authority that is required in your position. This is a self-paced program and God alone knows how long it will take.

Let me make one other thing very clear. This is a spiritual process, NOT an academic one. Some job seekers have mistakenly thought that their Kingdom job search could be accomplished by sitting at home, reading the Bible, and waiting for a new job to drop in. Nothing could be further from the truth. This is an on-the-job training process. You're probably going to work harder than you have ever worked before!

What can you tell me about my new Boss?

I'll let Him tell you Himself. This is a direct quote from one of His employee meetings:

> *"I tell you the truth, I am the gate for the sheep. . . . Those who come in through me will be saved, They will come and go freely and will find good pastures. The thief's purpose is to steal and kill and destroy. My purpose is to give them a rich and satisfying life. I am the good shepherd. The good shepherd sacrifices his life for the sheep. A hired hand will run when he sees a wolf coming. He will abandon the sheep because they don't belong to him and he isn't their shepherd. And so the wolf attacks them and scatters the flock. The hired hand runs away because he's working only for the money and doesn't really care about the sheep. I am the good shepherd; I know my own sheep, and they know me, just as my Father knows me and I know the Father. So I sacrifice my life for the sheep"* (John 10:7-15).

Did you get that part about the good pastures? He's telling us that He will lead his sheep (that's us) in and out of jobs, and will continuously care for us. Pastures are our workplaces. That's where we receive the resources we need in order to be productive. He promises to see to it that we'll learn to come and go freely and never be defeated by unemployment again. He really means it, too. He'll never leave you and He'll never take His eyes off your situation. If you come up against anything you can't handle, He'll be right there to back you up.

He's also a very hands-on manager. He expects all of His disciples to ask lots of questions and to keep Him involved in everything. He'll be happy to explain anything that might confuse you. He will also expect you to do what He tells you. He takes obedience very seriously and He's a great role model. He never does anything without His Father's direction. Your progress will be measured by your willingness and ability to do the same. He puts it like this: *"Those who accept my commandments and obey them are the ones who love me . . ."* (John 14:21), so *". . . if you abide in My word, you are My disciples indeed"* (John 8:31 NKJV). Study what Jesus does and copy Him. Probably the best way to start is to do everything you do on a foundation of love. That's how He's best known.

What am I going to be paid?

Here's a very brief summary of God's compensation and benefits plan for His disciples. If you go through His Word and research the words riches, prosperity, supply, and blessing, you'll develop a much better picture of the whole thing.

For starters, there's the "signing bonus." *"'I tell you the truth,' Jesus replied, 'no one who has left home or brothers or sisters or mother or father or children or fields* ***for me and the gospel*** *will fail to receive a hundred times as much in this present age (homes, brothers, sisters, mothers, children and fields—and with them persecutions) and in the age to come, eternal life'"* (Mark 10:29-30 NIV).

This is one of those scriptures that has been frequently taken out of context and used to justify greed and personal gain. Absent the study of God's Word, you too might think this Scripture promises an immediate hundredfold return in things and a guarantee of earthly wealth. **It does neither.**

Jesus is telling His disciples that if they lose their homes for the sake of the Gospel, they will be welcomed into a "hundred" homes of other believers and if they lose their families, they will find new brothers and sisters in the Body of Christ. It's also easy to skip right over the words "for me and the gospel" and "along with persecution."

Keep studying and you'll find that extraordinary provision will be made available to believers who are acting in the will of God in order to serve His purposes. Just don't confuse "provision" with money. God will provide what is needed in the circumstance to accomplish the purpose. But, the motive must be service to the Gospel and the heart must be willing to exchange self-interest and personal comfort for persecution, in order to qualify for this "bonus." After all, a signing bonus is not paid to everyone; it is available only to those who are willing to "give away all" and completely surrender to the will of God.

As for base pay, He promises to see to it that you "*lack no good thing*."[11] Just make sure you're working full time on the assign-

11. Psalm 34:10

ments set before you. My favorite compensation promise is 2 Corinthians 9:8: *"And God is able to make all grace abound to you, so that in all things at all times, having all that you need, you will abound in every good work"* (NIV). Do you see what the currency is here? It's the very grace of God! Paul tells us that he is confident that through God's grace we will have what we need to abound to every good work—in other words, to accomplish His purposes for us.

I have received payment on this promise of grace many times. I know God is able to meet our needs even when they appear impossible. I remember a time after I moved to Atlanta with my husband and two small children. We had been transferred by his company and I planned to remain self-employed but to work from home.

I was an executive recruiter at the time and figured that with my training and experience, all I needed was a telephone and a corporate bank account. I naively expected my business to be up and running immediately. Well, I struggled and the business struggled and the bills kept coming. Panic and terror parked themselves on my front porch and refused to leave. I began to believe that I had made a mistake that would lead to the financial ruin of my family.

I fell apart one morning after dropping my son off for preschool. While driving home, the waterworks started and I couldn't stop them. As I turned onto my street I cried out, "God, I need money today, to keep the phone and lights turned on and to pay my household bills."

I turned into my driveway and, seeing the mailbox, realized that I hadn't gotten yesterday's mail. There, in the mailbox, was a check for one thousand dollars. It was all the money I needed, right when I needed it. What amazed me was that God had started a process, weeks earlier, to get a check to me that morning. Months before that, He had arranged for there to be an excess in our mortgage escrow account so I would have money to pay these bills. That was no coincidence. It was just God doing what He promised, supplying all my needs "*according to His riches in glory by Christ Jesus*" (Philippians 4:19 NKJV).

The point of that story is not that God will put a check in your mailbox, but that He will always provide for your needs, often in some rather creative ways.

Money is not the only thing in God's pay plan, and it's not even the best provision. He also offers:

- ***Retirement benefits*** – "*I will be your God throughout your lifetime—until your hair is white with age. I made you, and I will care for you. I will carry you along and save you*" (Isaiah 46:4).

- ***Vacation benefits*** – "*Come to me, all of you who are weary and carry heavy burdens, and I will give you rest*" (Matthew 11:28).

- ***Work life Quality*** – "*Peace I leave with you, My peace I give to you*" (John 14:27 NKJV). "*You will keep him in perfect peace, Whose mind is stayed on You, Because he trusts in You*" (Isaiah 26:3 NKJV).

- ***Promotional Opportunities*** – "*Therefore humble yourselves under the mighty hand of God, that He may exalt you in due time, casting all your care upon Him, for He cares for you*" (1 Peter 5:6-7 NKJV).

- ***Supplies and Equipment*** — Because you are an alien and stranger to this world's economy, all of your provisions will come directly from God and you will want for nothing. *"And this same God who takes care of me will supply all your needs from his glorious riches, which have been given to us in Christ Jesus"* (Philippians 4:19).

- ***Health "Assurance"*** — *"Do not be wise in your own eyes; fear the LORD and shun evil. This will bring health to your body and nourishment to your bones"* (Proverbs 3:7-9 NIV).

Beyond all these provisions, there is simply no way to assign a value to the priceless gift we've been given in Jesus. What is it worth to you to have eternal life, forgiveness, and mercy? If God never gives you another thing, aren't you already blessed beyond measure?

Far too many believers have lost sight of all that we have been given and have turned toward the worldly treasures that rust and have no eternal value. It's my hope that I've shared enough of God's Word to convince you that there is nothing on earth that can compete with what He provides for you every moment of every day.

And, one more thing—the economy of God cannot be shaken. He isn't dependent on company profitability or affected in any way by current economic conditions. His is a never-ending supply. He's prepared to deliver everything you need as soon as you ask and put your confidence and trust in Him.

What can you tell me about citizenship in my new Kingdom?

Well, first of all, God's Kingdom is nothing like the world's kingdom to which you're accustomed. The law of this world is the law of sin and death. The Law of the Kingdom is the law of love and life. The values of this world are in direct opposition to those established by Christ. Look at just a few of the more obvious differences:

The world says...	The Word says...
"Stand up for your rights and look out for yourself."	"Lay down your life for Jesus' sake and you'll find it."
"Get whatever you can and hang onto it."	"Give and it will be given to you."
"Love things and use people."	"Use things and love people."

You get the idea. It's obvious that you won't learn the Kingdom way of life in today's educational system or by listening to the popular media. To accomplish what you're here to do, and to behave as a child of the King, you'll have to change your entire way of thinking. That will be the biggest challenge of your Kingdom job search.

If you're wondering how you'll learn this new way of life, Psalm 119:10-11 offers a clue: *"I seek you with all my heart; do not let me stray from your commands. I have hidden your word in my heart that I might not sin against you"* (NIV).

You will have to learn to walk in love and by faith, believing God's Word over what you see and what you've been taught to believe. This transformation process begins with an understanding of three foundational truths about the Kingdom of God.

The Kingdom of God Is Real

Too many of us have bought into the common delusion that if we can't touch, see or hear it, it must not exist. Believers everywhere act as if the Kingdom of God is imaginary, or at best, significantly less substantial and dependable than the natural realm.

I hear job seekers make statements like "I know what God has promised, but I need real answers to handle my real problems." Obviously, they don't understand reality. The truth is that the invisible spirit realm is real, permanent and eternal. This world, this "natural" realm is only a fleeting image masquerading as something permanent. One is eternal, the other but a blink of the eye. Which is more real?

Theologian Teilhard de Chardin nailed it when he declared that, "We are not human beings having a spiritual experience. We are spiritual beings having a human experience." It is our spirit that defines our true self.

Furthermore, God stands in eternity with a complete and perfect understanding of everything that has happened, is happening, or ever will happen. Many of us behave as if God can't see what's going on here, and it's up to us to point things out to Him. There's even a bumper sticker that says "God is my co-pilot." That makes me want to rush up to the driver and yell, "Quick, change seats!"

God is the only One who can see well enough to direct our lives.

In truth, God is the only One who can see well enough to direct our lives. When a pilot is flying an airplane he knows when the visibility is bad. That's when he makes the decision to fly by instrumentation. He can't see what governs the equipment but a wise pilot trusts those instruments more than he trusts his eyesight. We would do well to trust God as much. He has given us a measure of faith so that we can fly by divine instrumentation.

Imagine that! The Creator Himself is willing to lead us with His limitless wisdom and intelligence plus the perspective of timeless eternity! Trusting God over our natural senses is clearly the most reasonable thing we could ever do... and yet many believers find that idea dangerous.

The concept of time is another aspect of the sensory world that causes us problems. It amazes me when I hear believers say, "I don't think God is going to come through for me. I guess my prayers just didn't get to Him in time." That's just nonsense. God doesn't require time to get something done, for heaven's sake! Everything we will ever need in life already exists in that very real spirit realm we struggle to accept. God isn't telling us what might happen when He gives us an insight. He's telling us what He has already seen. Can you grasp how your life will be transformed when you understand the radically different Truth of the Kingdom?

The Kingdom of God Is Powerful

Not only is the Kingdom of God invisible and yet real, the Kingdom of God is powerful. The spiritual laws of God's Kingdom transcend the natural laws of this world. The Bible provides plenty of examples in which the spirit realm trumped gravity, time, travel, disease, and even death.

- Jesus may have started it, but Peter walked on water too (Matthew 14:29).
- It was Peter again who followed an angel right through prison walls to freedom (Acts 12:9).
- As Paul and Silas were praising God in their prison cell, an earthquake, that did no other reported damage, managed to shake open the locked cell doors (Acts 16:25-26).

- If a little boy's lunch was enough to feed thousands of hungry people (Matthew 14:17-21), you can have confidence that God is able to stretch scarce resources today.

- There's even an account in which Phillip finished baptizing a eunuch and was instantly transported to another city without the assistance of a plane, train or automobile! (Acts 8:39-40)

- A young man fell from a third story window and was brought back to life in time for dinner (Acts 20:9-11).

- The disciples found money for taxes in the mouth of a fish (Matthew 17:27). Just as easily, money can unexpectedly appear in a job seeker's mailbox when it's needed—if God so chooses.

So obviously, amazing things can happen—if it serves the will of God for a particular person at a particular time. In view of all that, how hard do you think it will be for God to thaw a hiring freeze or open a position for you? In the Kingdom of God, all these things are easy! Didn't our Lord promise this? We read in Mark 10:27 that "*Jesus looked at them intently and said, 'Humanly speaking, it is impossible. But not with God. Everything is possible with God.'*"

When believers understand this—I mean really grab onto it—this truth completely transforms the way they approach the workplace. Can you imagine the impact of an entire workforce moving in and out of assignments led by God Himself?

The Kingdom of God Is Ours!

The power of God is available to us right now, as we go about our daily lives. He loves us and He desires only good for us. Because of His love, and the finished work of Jesus, we can overcome every natural obstacle. We have guaranteed victory in every aspect of life, including work. We truly are "*more than conquerors.*"

But we will only achieve our position of authority through complete submission and obedience to God's will and the Kingdom way of life. That's why seeking the Kingdom of God is our starting point, and why it makes sense to settle the matter of accepting and acknowledging your Kingdom citizenship early in the job search process. There's simply no time to waste.

Don't worry if you can't do it "perfectly." It's not a one-time event, but a process at which we become better over time. I have Joshua 24:15 hanging on my living room wall. As I was contemplating those words the other day I discovered a new way to look at it. "*Choose for yourselves* ***this day*** *whom you will serve. . . .*" The choice has to be a daily decision. Before you go out each day you need to choose again whom you will serve as the day unfolds. Yes, you are a citizen of the Kingdom of God and a member of His royal family. That's the part God did for you. But the choice about how you will live and whose Law you will obey is up to you to decide each and every day.

You may be looking for a job or a new career, or perhaps your work is satisfying but your family life needs attention. Whatever your situation, you must never forget that you work for God. Nothing matters more than His eternal plan and the Kingdom assignments He has for you. Nothing will bring you more success and happiness in life than to live in the will of God. Nothing you do will make a greater difference in this world than your demonstration of Kingdom life. It's as if you've been invited to a new country to start a new life. Fortunately, there's a handbook for new citizens—the Bible. It will show you how to "ask, seek and knock" for new work and a new, victorious way of life.

CHAPTER FOUR

1. Why are believers told to seek the Kingdom of God first?

2. How do we seek the Kingdom and how will we know when we find it?

3. How is a Kingdom job search different from the world's way of looking for a job?

4. How does the economy of God compare to the economy of this world? (Identify similarities and differences.)

JOB SEEKER'S TIP #7 What Job Are You Looking For?

There are many right answers to this question and one really bad answer. Guess which category this one fits into: "I'll take any job right now; I'm not picky. I just want someplace secure with good benefits." Any variation that sounds like you have no direction, you're only interested in yourself, or that you consider yourself to be desperate, is a bad response.

Beyond that, here are some key elements that an interviewer is listening for:

- ***Are you able to match your objective with the credentials it requires?***
- ***Do you know enough about this organization to know what positions exist here?***
- ***Can you clearly communicate what you're looking for?***
- ***Do you have the employer in mind or is it all about you?***

To match objective with credentials:

Get job descriptions for the job or jobs that interest you. Go to www.bls.gov to review jobs in many categories and see the basic education, skills and experience they require. Online want ads are available in newspaper archives so you can review the education and experience sought by employers trying to fill specific positions. Best: Get an actual position description from the target company through a friend or contact there. Check what they list as requirements and pursue it ONLY if you possess the skills and experience listed. You may have fewer, or more, years of experience than they ask for, but you must be in the right ballpark in terms of skills and experience. If a degree is required, you may be able to substitute relevant experience for it. The specific type of degree listed is generally not that important.

Call and ask. If you have a contact there, this should be easy. If not, check the organization's website to see if you can find positions listed on a job posting page or a careers section. If all else fails, call the receptionist and ask for the (state the name) department. When you get someone in the department, ask "Do you have a (state the name) position in your department?" and "Is that the term you use for this position?" If there are similar or related positions, you can direct your energy toward them. But, there's no point in spending your energy where there are no opportunities for you.

To communicate your objective clearly:

Practice your response out loud. Be sure to stay somewhat broad in your answer and to identify one or two key skills that you want to use. Example: "Well, because I am fluent in Spanish and I have prior training experience in both design and delivery, I think a position in Training or a related HR generalist position, in Tampa or Miami, would allow me to make a good contribution."

To keep the employer in mind:

Look at the response above. Notice that it states the intention of making a good contribution and it highlights skills and experience an employer might be able to use. That's what you want to do. Don't ask for security, opportunity or benefits as you answer this question!

JOB SEEKER'S TIP #8 It's All About Trust

We have to trust God if we are going to allow Him to lead us. Similarly, an employer will have to trust you before bringing you into an employment relationship. People don't hire people they don't trust. That's not rocket science but it's true. It follows that you will want to earn the interviewer's trust as quickly as possible. Now, you may know that you are trustworthy and that you will be a blessing to anyone who hires you, but the employer doesn't know that. So you can just hope the employer will discover it quickly or you can do a few key things to proactively build trust.

BE-Attitudes for Creating Trust Quickly

Be friendly. Smile—on the phone, as well as in person. Believe it or not, your smile is actually audible. Let your smile light up your whole face! You have to actually mean that smile if you want it to show up in your eyes. If you're not a naturally friendly person, get busy building that attribute. There are plenty of opportunities in a job search to practice friendliness with strangers. *"For you will be treated as you treat others"* (Matthew 7:2).

Be positive. There is no excuse for being negative. Never bad-mouth a former employer. Never bad-mouth yourself! We all know that a negative person is likely to turn on us, too, the minute they're out of sight. There's no possibility for trust with people like that, is there? So let the words of your mouth, and the thoughts that you dwell on, be acceptable in the sight of the Lord (see Psalm 19:14).

Be considerate. Listen—really listen. If you're unclear about a question, rephrase it to ensure you understand what is being asked. When you've given an answer, ask if it met the interviewer's objective. ("Does that answer your question?") And watch the time. Don't overstay your welcome! Treat the interviewer as you would like to be treated. *"Love your neighbor as yourself"* (James 2:8).

Be true to your word. If you make any commitment, no matter how small, be sure to keep it. That means being on time, calling when you say you will and following through as planned. *"Simply let your 'Yes' be 'Yes,' and your 'No,' 'No'"* (Matthew 5:37 NIV).

Be of service. Find some simple way to provide a service for the other person. Send them an article they might find interesting, make an introduction to someone, share a resource or business lead. ***"Serve wholeheartedly, as if you were serving the Lord, not men"*** (Ephesians 6:7 NIV).

Be honest. Tell the truth about what you can and cannot do. *"People with integrity walk safely, but those who follow crooked paths will slip and fall"* (Proverbs 10:9).

CHAPTER 5

ASK

"Cry out for insight, and ask for understanding. Search for them as you would for silver; seek them like hidden treasures. Then you will understand what it means to fear the Lord, and you will gain knowledge of God."

– Proverbs 2:3-5

There are so many things believers need when they're out of work or their businesses are struggling, so it's a good thing that the "kingdom job search" process begins with Ask. First on the list for many job seekers is money to pay the bills and meet the day-to-day expenses of life. But money won't take care of everything. A successful job search requires guidance and training, confidence and presentation skill, employment leads and open positions, as well as timing and favor. Money can't buy these job search essentials. So, it ought to be a great relief to know that we can get whatever we need by asking—especially if the One being asked is God Himself! Just take a look at the promises we've been given:

> *"And whatever things you ask in prayer, believing, you will receive"* (Matthew 21:22 NKJV).

> *"You can ask for anything in my name, and I will do it, so that the Son can bring glory to the Father"* (John 14:13).
>
> *"I appointed you to go and produce lasting fruit, so that the Father will give you whatever you ask for, using my name"* (John 15:16).
>
> *"And since we know he hears us when we make our requests, we also know that he will give us what we ask for"* (1 John 5:15).

The directions seem simple enough. Just make a list, like children do at Christmas, hand the list to God, and everything will be delivered as requested. I used to think that was how it worked. Whenever I was out of work (or out of money) I would go to God and try to impress upon Him how necessary it was for Him to get busy on my behalf. I thought my prayers needed to be fervent (read that frantic and desperate) in order to get Him to drop whatever He was doing and help me out. I'm exaggerating a bit, but you get the idea.

My entire thought process was wrong, however. I was thinking in terms of this world and the way that it operates, not in terms of God's eternal and spiritual world. I began to understand that God stands outside of Time and has already established all that I would ever want or need. He counted the cost of bringing me into this life for a specific purpose and created all the provisions I would need to accomplish that plan.

This is what Jesus was talking about when He told His disciples: *"For your Father knows exactly what you need even before you ask Him"* (Matthew 6:8). We don't have to beg for God to do something for us. He's already taken care of it. Jesus concludes His teaching on this matter with our foundation Scripture:

> *"Therefore do not worry, saying, 'What shall we eat?' or 'What shall we drink?' or 'What shall we wear?' For after all these things the Gentiles seek. For your heavenly Father knows that you need all these things. But seek first the kingdom of God and His righteousness, and all these things shall be added to you"* (Matthew 6:31-33 NKJV).

But if we're not praying to tell God what we need, what then are we praying about? As you can see, this asking business is not as easy as it first appears. Across the years I've listened to countless job seekers express everything from anger and frustration to confusion and deep sadness when they talk about their experiences with prayer and asking. Matthew 21:22, *"And whatever things you ask in prayer, believing, you will receive,"* comes up so often and has caused such distress that I've named it God's Painful Promise!

The experiences shared are different each time but the questions are pretty much the same: How do we deal with the fact that we keep asking for work, yet we are still unemployed? That we ask for resources and the money doesn't come? That we seek opportunities and can't find them? That we go to companies and knock but they don't let us in? Does this sound familiar? Have you asked God for things you've needed and failed to receive them? If so, then you understand why the whole first phase of God's strategy is devoted to this critical issue.

I remember one evening, years ago, when all the members in my small group were struggling. We were praying, believing God would provide employment breakthroughs, and we were stuck. Absolutely nothing was happening for anyone in the group and discouragement had set in. It was an awful experience. Members of the group were speculating about the reasons things weren't working. Maybe God's promises were only for a select group of disciples. Maybe our faith wasn't strong enough. Maybe we didn't really believe, we just thought we did. Maybe God was answering and His answer was "No."

There was a lot of guessing but we found no real answers. Then, this Scripture came to mind: *"Cry out for insight, and ask for understanding. Search for them as you would for silver; seek them like hidden treasures. Then you will understand what it means to fear the Lord, and you will gain knowledge of God"* (Proverbs 2:3-5).

So we went to God with James 5:16, *"The effective, fervent prayer of a righteous man avails much"* (NKJV), and asked for wisdom. We had to find out what was required in order to pray and know, beyond a shadow of a doubt, that the prayer was going to produce results. That's when we began to gain an understanding about how to ask in line with the laws of the Kingdom.

Here's what we learned. First and foremost, requests need to be in the character of God. If God wouldn't be glorified by the result, if the Kingdom wouldn't be served, there's no reason to expect God to honor the request.

Look at the promises again. Note the words about bringing glory to the Father and producing lasting fruit for the Kingdom. A little investigation into the way Jesus put forth His requests sheds light on how to ensure our motives are right. *"I don't speak on my own authority. The Father who sent me has commanded me what to say and how to say it"* (John 12:49). If we ask God what to ask for, we can certainly be confident that our requests will be granted. But when we ask for what pleases us, with no thought of serving a greater or eternal purpose, chances are the request won't qualify for a divine response. And, unfortunately, should we get what we selfishly requested, the consequences may be as disastrous as those experienced by the prodigal son. Do you really want to end up in a pigpen?

From much personal experience, I can share a great method of making sure your prayers fail. When I first started praying with the Word of God and the name of Jesus, I didn't know the rules, so I approached the process like I was studying to be a magician. I figured if I could find a promise that agreed with my request, I could combine that promise with the name of Jesus. With a little practice, I would master the process of getting God to do as I asked. Imagine thinking that I had found the formula for making God do my will! That may seem ridiculous, but I'll bet I'm not the only one who's done it. How often do we claim things "In the Name of Jesus" as if it's a spiritual "abracadabra," only better?

In effect, I had been trying to use Jesus' name to buy things without His approval! I'd be pretty unhappy if my daughter took one of my credit cards and ran up a large bill without my permission. Yet that's what I was attempting to do with prayer. I finally learned that the power and authority He grants us is like a corporate line of credit to be used *for Kingdom purposes only*. To use the power of His name, He needs to approve our requests.

Again, the only way to know if our request meets with God's approval is to ask God what to ask for! What amazes me now is how generous and wonderful God is and how often He provides things just to delight us! Without even understanding how prayer worked, I have been blessed often through "faith accidents" that happened when I unknowingly lined up my requests with God's will. That's the wonderful thing about Kingdom laws—they always work. Always!

Here's another important understanding of how prayer works. God is not the great Dispenser and Withholder of Blessings. We have to let go of the idea that He manipulates us into behaving by bribing us with prayer answers when we're behaving properly, and withholding what we need when we're disappointing Him. In the spirit realm, God's inheritance has already been set aside for us in its entirety because of what Jesus has done! What a relief that our inheritance doesn't depend on the performance of the intended heir but on the One making the gift of it. That said, God is very clear in Galatians 4:1-2 that we cannot have access to our inheritance in any part until we are mature enough to manage it. *"Now I say that the heir, as long as he is a child, does not differ at all from a slave, though he is master of all, but is under guardians and stewards until the time appointed by the father..."* (NKJV). So our performance is not what causes God to be generous, His generosity is the result of His mercy. Our stewardship, on the other hand, does make a big difference. Every parent understands that you don't trust children with money until they demonstrate the maturity to handle it well. Why would we expect God to pour resources into us before we demonstrate the character and stewardship to manage them effectively?

Just come to God with an open, submitted heart and expect to receive the help you need.

God's answers don't come because somehow we've earned them either. Just as He isn't deciding each morning whether gravity will work today or if He'll make the sun come up, He isn't deciding whether to answer our requests or turn away from us based on the format of our prayers or our performance. Just come to God with an open, submitted heart and expect to receive the help you need. One other helpful hint: don't try to predict the response you'll get. God rarely answers in the manner we want or expect.

As we walk out this Kingdom employment strategy, we'll see spiritual laws working every time and all the time. What's really exciting is that we can learn how to identify and cooperate with them in alignment with the economy of God. That's when we'll see the powerful results of our prayers. Just as athletes win by learning how to play by the rules and master them, we will be victorious when we learn to *pray by the rules.*

In job and workplace ministries I have seen the greatest asking breakthroughs take place when believers examine and understand this verse:

> *"You ask and do not receive, because you ask amiss, that you may spend it on your pleasures"* (James 4:3 NKJV).

Other translations of the word "pleasure" are "lusts" (carnal, worldly desires), "passions" (emotional desires), and "evil, selfish motives." What we discovered was that our motives—the reasons for our requests—were tripping us up! In a way, it was good to find out that WE were the problem. After all, if we're causing the problem, we can stop what we're doing and change what we believe. That's a great deal better than believing that God's Word only works sometimes, or that the Enemy has the power to block God's promises (he doesn't). Over time and across various small groups, this clear picture emerged: When we ask only from the world's point of view, we ask incorrectly. Effective asking will always be based on Kingdom motives and serve Kingdom purposes.

Here are three common errors that job seekers make when they approach God with a prayer request —

1. They ask for things that won't solve the problem or meet the real need.

2. They unknowingly ask for something wrong or harmful.

3. They ask for something they already have.

Let's take a look at the first error—asking for things that won't solve the problem. In our earlier discussion about the Kingdom of God, recall that we acknowledged God alone as the One who sees well enough to direct our lives perfectly. When we forget that, we definitely ask amiss.

A classic example of asking for something that won't solve the real problem occurs when job seekers realize that money is getting tight and there's no job in sight. Someone tells them to "just take any job," and they race out to do just that. Highly trained professionals, executives and managers start applying for whatever jobs they can find. Soon they're praying "Lord, just give me this job," begging for a position that doesn't fit them in the slightest! This is textbook "asking amiss"!

Obviously fear is at the root of that request—fear that money will run out and bills won't get paid. But, believing that an inappropriate job is the right solution and then asking God to provide it is fundamentally wrong. If we need provision, then we should ask God for provision. If we are facing a problem, our request should be for wisdom and guidance to discover what God has in mind and how to cooperate with His plan.

Years of observing countless job searches have confirmed that any time we assess a problem on our own, come up with a solution, and ask God to do it our way, we are going to fail. I can't say it any plainer than that. Look at the belief behind this behavior. Isn't this a public statement that God cannot do what He promised or that we know better than He does? It's only when believers become convinced that God really won't provide abundant life that they decide to take matters into their own hands. On more than a few occasions I've heard job seekers say, "I have to do something. God isn't talking so I'm just going to do this and see what happens. With any luck God will show up and help me get the job." With any *luck*? What's wrong with that picture?

There's an important sidebar to this topic. Look at the many things wrong with the "take any job you can find" solution. You may hear this frequently from well-meaning advisors—people in whom you place much faith and trust—but it is absolutely terrible advice!

First of all, consider the employer. When someone fills a job, the employer invests energy and resources training that person to be productive in his business. That employer deserves an employee who is excited about the position, wants to be there, and isn't planning on leaving as soon as a better offer comes along. Any job seeker who takes a position without making a whole-hearted commitment to the new employer is using that employer for selfish motives.

Consider now the job seeker who needs, and is appropriately qualified for, that lower-level position. He will not be able to get his job because it's been taken by a person less suited, who doesn't really want the job, and who doesn't plan on staying. So a selfish action that takes advantage of an employer also potentially harms another job seeker.

Further, the overqualified worker who took the wrong position cannot now search effectively for an appropriate job because the "take anything" job uses up all available work time. It's very likely that the stop-gap job won't even cover his bills, not even meeting the need it was supposed to satisfy. This is more than an error—it's a trap! If fear makes you take a job that you clearly do not fit, just remember that God does not use fear as a motivator. And, it just might be a snare.

Now please don't misunderstand me—there's nothing wrong with a short-term or part-time job, a temporary assignment, or a contractor opportunity. There's also nothing wrong with dropping back to a lower level in order to learn a new line of work. But the take-whatever-you-can-get mentality is not driven by a Kingdom motive. If you're confused about your options and can't resolve the question "Is this God's idea, my idea or the Enemy's?" it means you need to keep growing in your relationship with God. But here's a great tip in the meantime: If fear suggests a way to go, do the opposite. Fear will never lead you to the will of God. When you simply don't know what to do, ask God for His will and wait until you are directed to do something. Peace and confidence will accompany His direction.

It's also easy to ask for the wrong thing. This happened in my very first small group and I have never forgotten the request, nor God's surprising answer. Eight of us decided to conduct a 30-day prayer experiment. We planned to meet every week for one month and pray for each other every day. Each person in the group had one specific request to bring before the Lord. About half of the group had requests related to work.

Ted, my assigned prayer partner, wanted a new job in retail jewelry. At the time he was a tire store supervisor who wanted to become a jeweler, so he clearly needed God's involvement. When we met one week later, some group members already had good news to report. Ted had made no progress, but he was committed to waiting on the Lord for an opportunity. Week two brought more of the same. Everyone except Ted could see visible evidence of God intervening on their behalf. Some had interviews, others were experiencing improved relationships but nothing was happening for Ted.

The third meeting went the same way and now we had only one

more week for our "experiment." Finally I asked Ted, "Do you really want to be a jeweler? Is this really your heart's desire?" To everyone's surprise, his eyes filled with tears and he said, "No. I don't want to leave my job. I love what I do and I love where I work." So what did he really want God to do for him? "I want to stay right where I am," he said, "and I want God to move everyone else out. The people who work for me are lazy and difficult to manage, and my boss doesn't support me or care about the quality of work being done." That was his true desire. But since he couldn't see any way for that to happen he went after the next best thing. Ted had decided that God couldn't or wouldn't give him what he really wanted, so he offered God a trade-off. Not surprisingly, God didn't take him up on it.

So, with one week of the experiment left, we all prayed for God to act on Ted's behalf, however He chose to do so. The next week Ted showed up with a stunned look on his face. That week his regional manager had called him to announce that a new branch would be opening nearby. They had decided to move Ted's boss and all his subordinates to the new location. Ted was being promoted to the manager's position and would have to hire an entirely new group of workers. He got everything he asked for with a promotion and raise thrown in for good measure! The lesson learned? When we simply tell God what we are feeling and express our needs, He'll take care of the rest. Again, our part is to ask and listen; His part is to determine the outcome.

...Our part is to ask and listen, His part is to determine the outcome.

Finally, we've probably all had failures because we've asked God for something He has already given us. Asking God for faith, for example, is an unnecessary request because the Word tells us ". . . *God has dealt to each one a measure of faith*" (Romans 12:3 NKJV). We just need to exercise the faith we already have in order to make it stronger.

All of this may be something you already know, or it could be a revelation that changes the nature of your experience from this point forward. All I can say is, if your past experience has been less than successful, please open your mind and heart anew. I know it's hard to forget the past and start fresh when you've experienced the frustration and pain of getting no results from your prayers. But that's what it's going to take.

Forget that you've asked and been disappointed. Forget thinking you don't have what it takes to get your prayers answered. Forget thinking these are nice promises that don't really work. Be willing to start over.

The Enemy has a good time taunting us about our prayer failures. He'd love for us to decide that God can't be trusted to meet our needs. More than that, he'd like believers to quit asking altogether, to simply quit praying. But, when we get fully into God's Word, learn how His Kingdom works, and listen for His voice, we'll finally discover the awesome gift we've been given through prayer.

Now let's look at some really good employment-type questions to ask of God. First and foremost, this is the perfect time to ask about your design. It's also a great time to identify your skills and talents and to ask for God's help to find work you will love to do. It makes sense to ask the Maker about your design features. He can tell you how to make the best use of your gifts and talents. After the shock of job loss, many job seekers need confirmation that their design is good and that they actually have gifts. Everyone needs to resolve this personal value issue before beginning an actual job search. It's difficult, if not impossible, to sell a product you don't believe in.

SEE JOB SEEKER'S TIP #9: "Tell Me About Yourself"

David joined our group a few years ago. He was generally quiet and consistently pessimistic. He reminded me of Eeyore from *Winnie the Pooh*. I think his motto was "Every silver lining has a cloud." This man struggled mightily with his job search and became more and more depressed each week. Still, he maintained that he was doing all that could be done.

Initially, David didn't want me to review his resume or practice interviews with him but, after months of unsuccessful searching, he reluctantly gave me his resume. When I read it, I was floored. In his Personal Summary, he described himself as a "high energy sales personality with a flair for the innovative." Nothing could have been further from the truth!

I'm not known for subtlety, so I called him on it. I asked David if he honestly thought that description fit him. Of course, he said "No, not really." Then he continued, "If I describe the way I really am, no one will ever hire me. I had a professional writer prepare my resume, and he said this is what people want."

How tragic. He believed that his personal design was inherently flawed. No wonder he was so negative. Then I asked David to describe his ideal job. He wanted an operations position in healthcare. Despite his background in the field, he was having no success generating interest. Well, no surprise there. Who would want an operations manager with a "high energy sales personality?"

The more we talked, the more David realized that his natural personality, skills and interests made him a great candidate for the work he wanted to do. So we changed his resume to reflect his true design. As he practiced describing his talents and skills, his whole demeanor changed. He put his new resume out in the market and within two weeks he was called for an interview. It went very well and he was hired shortly thereafter. The new job was an Operations Manager position, just as he had hoped.

The lesson is simply that God created every one of us and we are "fearfully and wonderfully made." There is some type of work that every one of us can do with excellence. When we find it, we also find joy in our work. Until job seekers are convinced they have gifts to offer the workplace, they will never be able to sell themselves.

What's your design? Are you proud of it? Would God like the way you describe yourself, His creation and beloved child? I'll even go a step further and propose a Job Search Commandment that says: "Thou shalt not go into a workplace you know little about, in a way you know nothing about, with a product you cannot effectively represent."

Job seekers need to ask not only about themselves and what they have to offer, but also about the job search process and how to master it. I don't understand why so many people run out into the market with no preparation, as if the process is a "piece of cake." I assure you, it's not. There are rules to this game and no one is born knowing them. The ability to search for and secure a job is a learned set of skills that comes only with training and practice.

As a representative of the Kingdom of God who is hoping to land a great job, you owe it to yourself to study this process and master it. We'll get into this more deeply in the Seek phase, but for now just know that Kingdom job seekers should demonstrate excellence. Research the marketplace, prepare a resume that represents you accurately and professionally, and practice all the presentation skills required.

"Work hard so you can present yourself to God and receive his approval. Be a good worker, one who does not need to be ashamed and who correctly explains the word of truth" (2 Timothy 2:15). Remember, God is your employer and He has assigned you to a Kingdom job search. Make sure you are conducting the process in a way He will approve.

This is also a great time to gain clarity about your assignment and destiny. Not surprisingly, God's purpose has nothing to do with the world's concept of career development. God is in the people development business. There's nothing Kingdom-like about sacrificing families and friendships to build a successful career. Creating a business empire and striving to make all the right moves in order to further one's career and garner success is the way the world does things. When personal gain, reputation, money, and prestige are our top priorities, we cannot expect God to bless our efforts. Not only that, but in seeking these worldly objectives we will also never experience fulfillment and satisfaction.

I've heard job seekers express concern that if they surrender to God's will and accept their destiny, He might ask them to do something they don't want to do. What if God wants them to minister in an impoverished area or do work that puts them in harm's way. What if God's plan includes shipwrecks or prison or even stoning; how could they possibly surrender to that? In response I invite them to study how Paul felt about the assignment he'd been given, or Nelson Mandela or Mother Theresa. Did they complain about their destinies…can we find any evidence they were sorry they chose to wholly follow God?

In 1 Corinthians 9:22-25, Paul says, "*I have become all things to all men so that by all possible means I might save some. I do all this for the sake of the gospel, that I may share in its blessings. Do you not know that in a race all the runners run, but only one gets the prize? Run in such a way as to get the prize. Everyone who competes in the games goes into strict training. They do it to get a crown that will not last, but we do it to get a crown that will last forever*" (NIV). What this tells me is that, no matter what the assignment entails, if we are in God's perfect will we will be blessed eternally and completely fulfilled and satisfied in it. Charles Spurgeon says it this way, "He who affirms that Christianity makes men miserable, is himself an utter stranger to it. It were strange indeed if it made us wretched, for see to what a position it exalts us! It makes us sons of God. Suppose you that God will give all the happiness to His enemies, and reserve all the mourning for His own family? . . . Shall the sinner, who has no part in Christ, call himself rich in happiness, and we go mourning as if we were penniless beggars? . . . We have the earnest of our inheritance in the comforts of the Spirit, which are neither few nor small."

God's purpose will always be based in love. It will always bring Him glory and give us joy and satisfaction as we serve others.

Finally, despite the concern of many believers who are looking for work, there is no need to struggle to find your real purpose, nor is there any need to wait to discover it before looking for your next work assignment. God's purposes can be accomplished in every environment and every type of work. You needn't fear missing God or taking a wrong step. We have the failure-proof promise of our Good Shepherd that He will lead us in and out of good pastures. We can trust Him to order our steps if we are actively seeking His direction. It's perfectly safe to take action as the Spirit leads and ask God to show us how to bring the Kingdom with us wherever we go.

A season away from the workplace is the best time to learn how God wants to co-create with us. I'm reminded of a story I heard about George Washington Carver. In a time of prayer he had asked God, "What's the purpose of the universe?" God answered him saying, "Ask a smaller question." At his next question God responded with, "Ask a better question." On the third go-around God said, "Ask a practical question." So Carver asked about his research, "What can I do with a peanut?"

That's when God responded with hundreds of practical ideas. So, if you have a dream to make the world a better place by running a business, building a day-care center, counseling troubled youth or doing whatever you have in your heart, you can bring that dream to God and ask for His input and involvement. You and God can become close, personal friends during this season of unemployment. You can also become business partners and have a great time working together to bring your dreams to fruition. *"Take delight in the Lord, and he will give you your heart's desires"* (Psalm 37:4). This Scripture means more than most people realize and it removes confusion about the term "heart's desire." As we come into a close personal relationship with Jesus, delighting in Him, He will actually put desires into our hearts—desires that will bring us both great joy. Then, as we pray for the realization of those dreams and desires, He will bring them to fulfillment. We are satisfied as the Kingdom of God is served! It doesn't get better than that.

As we wrap up this discussion on Asking, let's take a moment to consider one other instruction. Jesus told His disciples, *"You can pray for anything, and if you have faith, you will receive it"* (Matthew 21:22). Another translation says that we must "pray, believing." (Remember, as already noted, that prayers should be in accordance with the purposes of God and that you should seek the things that glorify Him.) When we don't receive an answer to our prayer, we might also need to examine our belief and confidence in the Word of God. Jesus demonstrated the perfect way to make sure this isn't a problem for us.

Remember Jairus and the direction Jesus gave him when he got the report that his daughter had died? *"As soon as Jesus heard the word that was spoken, He said to the ruler of the synagogue, 'Do not be afraid; only believe'"* (Mark 5:36 NKJV).

Jesus directed Jairus to make a firm, quality decision to turn away from all fear and doubt and stay fixed on God. If we want answers to our prayers, that's the kind of decision we'll have to make. Here's what a quality decision looks like. My mother watches a popular TV game show every evening. She knows the channel that carries the program and the time slot when it airs. One night she asked me to turn the show on for her, and I couldn't find it. I told her that the show must have been preempted by some other program that night because it wasn't on. Her response was one of flat denial; I had to be wrong. She came into the living room, took the remote control from me and found the show, just as she said she would. She had definitely decided what she believed and would not be persuaded otherwise.

We need to have unshakable belief in the Kingdom of God and His faithfulness to "draw near to us when we draw near to Him" with our needs and questions; to become so convinced that He will provide for us and guide us that nothing will change our minds about it. But, let me add something here for new believers especially. Don't worry if you're not able to be this resolved yet. The key to answered prayer is NEVER found in us! You can cry out "Jesus!" anytime, anywhere and He will answer. Look how He responded to the father who cried out, *"I do believe; help me overcome my unbelief!"* (Mark 9:24 NIV). Simple faith in Jesus is all it will ever take. The firm resolve part is for our benefit—it saves us a lot of wasted thought and energy and keeps us focused on the right thing, listening for God's answer.

It's also important to know that to be fully persuaded we have to receive God's promises personally. When God quickens a promise in our hearts, as we study His Word, we can take that promise to the bank.

Unfortunately, for far too many people, God's promises are just something they've heard about and too often, as part of erroneous teaching. Everywhere we turn we can hear people quoting promises from the Word and telling listeners that they can be used to "attract" whatever they want, whenever they want it. Jesus never said anything like that. In fact, in John 12:49, He declares quite the opposite: *"For I have not spoken on My own authority; but the Father who sent Me gave Me a command, what I should say and what I should speak"* (NKJV). We need to follow Jesus' example, stay in His Word continuously and listen to hear His specific, personal answers to all our questions.

Years ago there was another game show in which contestants were positioned with carts at the front of a store and turned loose for a shopping spree. I really admired the people who had the forethought to race toward the high-ticket items, filling their carts first with items of greatest value. What a great model for job seekers to follow when it comes to asking for things from God! Why don't we treat God's promises as blank checks that have been given to us and set out to spend them on the most valuable requests first?

Here are a few of those promises and some prayer requests to go after the "big ticket" items:

God's Promise – *"And since we know he hears us when we make our requests, we also know that he will give us what we ask for"* (1 John 5:15).

> **Our Request** – "Lord, bring me into a closer relationship with you. Grant me the ability to know you and to hear your voice clearly above all the noise in my life."

God's Promise – *"And whatever things you ask in prayer, believing, you will receive"* (Matthew 21:22 NKJV).

> **Our Request** – "Lord, give me eyes to see, ears to hear, and the ability to understand and discern your Kingdom laws and your will for my life. Show me how to walk in your love as a citizen of your Kingdom."

God's Promise – *"You can ask for anything in my name, and I will do it, so that the Son can bring glory to the Father"* (John 14:13).

> **Our Request** – "Lord, help me to follow the leading of the Holy Spirit within me. Make me instantly and completely obedient to your instructions so that I, too, might bring you glory."

God's Promise – *"I appointed you to go and produce lasting fruit, so that the Father will give you whatever you ask for, using my name"* (John 15:16).

> **Our Request** – "Lord, show me how you've made me and what

I have to offer. Help me use my gifts to bring your Kingdom into this world and to share your blessing wherever I go."

God's Promise — "*And so I tell you, keep on asking, and you will receive what you ask for. Keep on seeking, and you will find. Keep on knocking, and the door will be opened to you. For everyone who asks, receives. Everyone who seeks, finds. And to everyone who knocks, the door will be opened*" (Luke 11:9-10).

Our Request – "Lord, I give you my job search and everything about it. Tell me what to ask for, show me where to look, and send me to the doors that you want me to knock upon. I trust that your plan is perfect and ask that your will be done in my life."

Every one of those prayers comes from a *Kingdom motive* and aligns perfectly with the will of God. With requests like those, we can have complete confidence that our job search will be successful and the results more wonderful than we can imagine because "*The earnest prayer of a righteous person has great power and produces wonderful results*" (James 5:16).

Once your heart is fixed on God, you are ready to get out into the marketplace and start searching. The foundation has been laid, and we know the basic rules of the game. We've got the greatest coach in the Holy Spirit, and God has provided a complete playbook. As we begin the Seek phase of the process, we'll put all that we've learned into practice.

The Christian Worker's Creed is a summary of the things we've covered up to this point in our Kingdom job search and career journey. I pray it will bless you and provide you with a foundation to build upon.

The Christian Worker's Creed

I believe...

in God who is Love; Who is good and only good; Jesus who has given me victory in life; The Holy Spirit who dwells in me to guide and empower me.

I believe...

that unemployment will be a season of great blessing for me, and when my job search is over I will have: a deeper, richer relationship with God; a clearer appreciation for, and love of, my design; a greater capacity to love with the love of Christ; freedom from fear; and a new position where I will prosper and be a blessing.

I believe...

that I work for God to bring Him glory, that God is my provider and all my needs are met, that love is the foundation for my success, that faith in the Word produces results, that my gifts and talents are of great value, and that I am bringing God's Kingdom into the workplace.

CHAPTER FIVE

1. What keeps believers from receiving what they pray for?

2. How does God respond to prayers? (Does He ever ignore them or say "No"?)

3. What are good things for job seekers to pray for?

4. Has God ever answered your prayers? If yes, what did you ask for and what were your motives for the prayers?

JOB SEEKER'S TIP #9 Tell Me About Yourself

This question is something of a set-up. Interviewers may phrase the question this way, but they most assuredly do NOT want to hear all about you and your life. The best way to understand their point of view, and what they are really asking, is to rephrase the question like this: **"Please tell me information about yourself that will quickly let me know if I want to consider you for my open position."**

That means you need to stick to your professional experiences in the world of work, or at school, and you must lead off with the information that is most important for the job you're going to discuss. Now, here's what it takes to excel in answering this question—**Match your response to the listener's communication style.** You will make a strong first impression and a good connection if you use the style most comfortable for the interviewer.

There are four basic communication styles and each style listens from its particular point of view. Now, because you won't know each interviewer's style, you'll have to do the next best thing. Answer the question in a way that will satisfy all four styles.

1. **Thinkers** want to know that you are orderly and logical; they are listening for a balanced view of your past, present and future.

2. **Feelers** want to know that you relate well interpersonally; they are listening for a sense of who you are as a person, not just as a worker.

3. **Sensors** want to know that you can deliver results; they are listening for the facts and the "bottom line."

4. **Intuitors** want to know the "big picture" and how your work experiences fit together; they are listening for future plans, aspirations and ideas.

Example:

"Would it be all right if I started with an overview of my current work experience and my skills, then my education, and finally the reason I am interested in your open position?" **(A stated, orderly, logical introduction for Thinkers)**

Now wait for a response, establish eye contact and smile. **(Strong interpersonal skills for Feelers)**

"I am currently an administrative assistant supporting two managers in the IT department. I handle all the meetings, travel, presentation production and supply ordering for a group of five technical associates and the two managers. I've been in that position for three years and have strong proficiencies in Word, Excel, PowerPoint and Access. My performance ratings have all been in the category of Meets & Exceeds Expectations." **(Evident results for Sensors)**

"I have an associate's degree in English from Everest University. I am interested in your position because it is an Executive Assistant supporting a Vice President and I am trying to build my administrative career. I believe that administrative support is a valuable profession and I am committed to providing excellence in that field." **(Big picture, future focus for Intuitors)**

Your goal is to provide a glimpse into your background that is accurate and succinct. This format will give you the added advantage of communicating with style!

JOB SEEKER'S TIP #10

Prove It!

Never say, "There's no way to prepare for an interview because I don't know what questions I'll be asked." The questions aren't the issue. The questions in an interview are generally predictable, but that's not what guides good interview preparation. Your biggest preparation challenge is to know what you have to offer. **Your task is to become excellent at presenting YOU!** We know that the best indicator of future behavior is past behavior. So, if you want the interviewer to KNOW that you can do what you claim, you need to let her see when you've performed a skill or demonstrated some attribute in the past. Your goal is to create a mental YouTube video of your performance in your mind and then play it back for the interviewer.

The key to a **high performance interview** is the **CAR!** For each skill or attribute that you want to illustrate, use this simple format. First, tell the **C**onditions you faced, then the **A**ctions you took, and finally the **R**esult you achieved. Recall the direction of 2 Timothy 2:15: *"Be diligent to present yourself approved to God, a worker who does not need to be ashamed"* (NKJV).

Putting your CAR stories together:

1. Ask the Holy Spirit to help you recall the situations and examples you need as you prepare your CAR stories.

2. Pick a favorite accomplishment from school or work and tell the story. Then determine what that story proves or reveals about you. Use that story when asked about those skills and attributes.

3. Look at the skills and attributes you identified in your self-assessment exercises. Identify the attributes most likely to be of interest to the interviewer based upon the open position. Write a CAR story for each of those attributes.

4. Don't struggle to find big accomplishments or dramatic stories. Evidence of day-to-day consistency, excellent attendance and punctuality, and solid work performance is the type of background most employers are seeking.

5. Write down your CAR stories and **practice saying them out loud.** You won't know how you're going to sound in the interview if you don't practice out loud. Record your voice and play it back to hear how you sound to others.

6. Prepare one good CAR example for every skill or attribute you claim to have. If you can't prove it, you don't have it.

7. Keep your CAR examples as brief as possible. (Ninety seconds is a good rule of thumb.) Let the interviewer ask for more information if it's needed.

CHAPTER 6

SEEK

"Trust in the Lord with all your heart; do not depend on your own understanding. Seek his will in all you do, and he will show you which path to take."

– Proverbs 3:5-6

"But those who trust in the Lord will find new strength. They will soar high on wings like eagles. They will run and not grow weary. They will walk and not faint."

– Isaiah 40:31

My husband learned to swim the day his father tossed him out of their fishing boat and then rowed a little more than an arm's length ahead of him all the way back to shore. Granted, this wasn't the kindest, gentlest way to teach swimming, but it was effective.

The Seek phase of a Kingdom job search is a pretty similar experience. Right now you may be far from shore in very deep water. By the time you make land you may well be strong and proficient in every aspect of this job search process, both spiritual and natural.

Or, you may be only a short distance from your next assignment right now. You might be in the unemployment water just long enough to try out some Kingdom principles and learn a few, basic things about looking for a job.

Unfortunately, no one but God knows how long a job seeker will be "swimming." While that may make us uncomfortable, it's just a fact of life. I'm pretty sure Moses had no idea he'd be in the wilderness with his crowd for 40 years! Joseph probably wasn't planning on a decade-long detour in prison on his way to God's promise either. Job didn't know, in his season of testing, when, or if, it would ever end. But every one of them made it through, and so will you.

Let's go back to Job for a minute. We're all probably familiar with his story, but look at how it expressed God's confidence in him. Clearly Job knew nothing of that conversation between God and the devil concerning him. I'm sure he had no idea that all of heaven and hell were watching to see how he would respond to his challenging circumstances. But knowing everything that Job would experience, God also knew that Job would stand strong. So here's my question—what if Job's story is not a one-time event in history? What if there are others God is holding up as a taunt to the devil? What if you're one of them? Imagine God watching as Satan took your job away and then immediately sending him a text message: "Nice try, but your plan won't work. This believer is going to grow in faith and Christ-likeness throughout the job search process. You're going to be sorry you messed with this one!"

I can assure you that your job search process will end. This is not a permanent condition. When it's over you'll look back on how you handled this season of your life. So decide right now if you want to go through this time kicking and screaming or if you want to go in the strength of the Lord and in His mighty power.

Personally, as I went through my toughest times, I did a fair amount of whining and had more than my share of pity parties. Looking back now, I can see how unnecessary that was. As soon as it ended I wished I had made more intentional decisions about how I wanted to behave while I was unemployed. As I watch many others journey through the season of joblessness I see that, for the most part, we have completely forgotten the idea of living to please God. This saddens me. Here we are, a people saved, forgiven, redeemed, and blessed by Christ Jesus who died for us, and we don't think about living in obedience simply out of gratitude for all that He has already done for us. There is such joy to be had in delighting someone we love. As you walk out this journey, I encourage you to behave in a manner pleasing to God and notice what a difference it will make when you put your head down on your pillow at night.

This will be a challenging season, but I encourage you to determine how you intend to respond to it at the start. Then, for the duration of your job search, behave as if you know that all the angels in heaven and demons in hell are watching you. Make sure you're giving the angels plenty to cheer about! It won't change the way that God views you or the support He'll provide for you. It will, however, enable you to feel really good about yourself and your witness for the Kingdom of God when it's all behind you. You cannot choose when the process will end, but you most definitely can choose how you'll handle the experience while you're in it.

This will be a challenging season, but I encourage you to determine how you intend to respond to it at the start.

One thing is certain, every one of your Kingdom assignments will last until you have completed all that God wants you to accomplish. Remember, God always has much more planned for you than just a quick reentry into the workplace. He's got those five blessings ready for you to claim. When I say this to job seekers the first time, you should see their faces. I tell them that God really wants to deliver all of His Kingdom blessings and most of them actually grimace. It's so hard for them to imagine that anything matters more than getting back to work as fast as possible.

If that's how you feel right now, don't be concerned. Multiple blessings don't take longer than single blessings. The length of a search is dependent on many things, including the time required to arrange and orchestrate our blessings by positioning the right people in the right places to receive us.

God also allows for the time it takes us to complete His assignments away from the workplace, as we'll discuss in a future chapter. Length of time is not the important thing about this season because you will never be left alone or without His provision as His will unfolds. God is your employer and your pay plan is assured. You can receive His compensation by faith in His Word, long before you land in your next assignment. The God who called you to His Kingdom is more than able to sustain you throughout your journey. He also is within an arm's reach at all times.

"Fear not, for I am with you."

We looked at this Scripture earlier but it might be helpful to see it again: *"Fear not, for I am with you. Be not dismayed, for I am your God. I will strengthen you, Yes, I will help you, I will uphold you with my righteous right hand"* (Isaiah 41:10 NKJV).

I am reminded again of Peter's famous water-walking experience. His faith got him a few steps out, but when he faltered and began to sink, Jesus was right there. Jesus immediately reached out and grabbed him. "'*You have so little faith,' Jesus said. 'Why did you doubt me?*'" (Matthew 14:31).

I'm pretty sure you will have moments of doubt along the way. Just keep that picture in mind when you feel yourself going under. Jesus will catch you if you call to Him. He'll never let you sink, however shaky your faith might be. Hopefully, as you practice standing against fear and doubt, those sinking moments will be few and far between. As you can see, the Seek phase of the job search is a huge challenge. You're going to be learning new job search skills and new Kingdom behaviors at the same time. Heaven, hell and everyone you know will be watching. It's like having to learn your solo in front of a huge audience, but it can be done with the empowerment of the Holy Spirit. In case you are wondering what you should accomplish in this orientation phase of your job search, aim at meeting the following objectives:

- Establish and adhere to a daily schedule that covers job search, personal, spiritual and volunteer activities.

- Produce a resume that accurately presents your skills and experience while conveying a bit of your personality.

- Develop an effective answer to each of the following questions: "Why are you unemployed?" "What are you looking for?" and "Tell me about yourself."

- Prepare one CAR story (see Job Seekers Tip) to prove every skill or attribute you claim to have. Practice relating your stories out loud.

- Gather a list of names and contact information for everyone you know.

- Locate a support group or professional mentor to provide feedback on your self-presentation.

As you go through this process you're not exempt from all the tasks of daily life, either. There are short-term projects for you to accomplish at home, relationships to maintain and the responsibilities of life to deal with. To help you handle all those demands, I'd like to propose a set of Job Search Commandments.

I use the term "commandments" with great care, because people often bristle at being commanded to do anything. Many have the idea that commandments are just someone's attempt to control them for ulterior, evil purposes. But I remember teaching my kids to "Freeze" when I called out that command. I just wanted them to stop instantly, for the sake of their own safety. These job search commandments are like that. They're offered because they have guided many job seekers through uncharted job search waters and kept them from harm. Some will sound pretty familiar to you by now. Others will break new ground. I can promise that all of them will be useful as you get out into the marketplace and begin to practice new skills and a Kingdom way of life.

Career Commandments

1. You shall seek God first.

2. You shall not fear.

3. You shall "pray according to the rules."

4. You shall work hard.

5. You shall let go of the past.
6. You shall love and take no offense.
7. You shall give and sow seed.
8. You shall walk by faith.
9. You shall give thanks.
10. You shall represent the Kingdom.

You shall seek God first. Why do we need to seek Him first? Many believers, including job seekers, seem to think it does something for God. They'll say things like, "I want to make God happy" or "I know God expects us to seek Him." We don't say it like we're talking about a love interest or a beloved child. Can you imagine saying, "I know I should call the one I'm in love with" or "It would make my precious daughter happy so I guess I ought to spend some time with her." Nonsense. We call and spend time with the special people in our lives because we love them and we want to be with them. It is the same in our relationship with God. He loves us. Amazing as it might be, Almighty God, the Creator of All, wants to be with us! He has wonderful things to tell us and His love to give us.

Somehow we have to make the shift from viewing our relationship with God as a spiritual assignment to a spiritual rendezvous that is the best part of our day. We fail to realize that God's love is the power source behind the entire Kingdom of God and all creation. The more we are filled with it, the more powerful we become. Ephesians 3:16-19 puts it this way, *"I pray that from his glorious, unlimited resources he will empower you with inner strength through his Spirit. Then Christ will make his home in your hearts as you trust in him. Your roots will grow down into God's love and keep you strong. And may you have the power to understand, as all God's people should, how wide, how long, how high, and how deep his love is. May you experience the love of Christ, though it is too great to understand fully. Then you will be made complete with all the fullness of life and power that comes from God."*

Do you see how God's love affects us? When we come to know the love of Christ, then we will be filled with the fullness of God and we will be complete, lacking nothing. God, who is able to do absolutely everything we can possibly dream of, desires to release His power in and through us. He wants us to seek Him first so He can put fuel in our tanks and give us everything we need to face the challenges of the day.

You shall not fear. I wish I could tell you that the enemy would be satisfied to simply get you out of a job. Unfortunately, he wants to keep you from serving the Kingdom. So he's still got his eye on you, and he always will as long as you're working on Kingdom assignments. This means you need to have your eye on him too. There's a line in Nehemiah 4:17-18 that describes the way God's people had to work while they were under threat of attack: *"Those who carried materials did their work with one hand and held a weapon in the other, and each of the builders wore his sword at his side as he worked"* (NIV).

That's how we need to approach the job search. Carry your resume and other job search materials and build your networks, but never put down the sword of the Spirit and never go out without the spiritual armor of God. *"Stay alert! Watch out for your great enemy, the devil. He prowls around like a roaring lion, looking for someone to devour"* (1 Peter 5:8).

You'll want to become excellent at recognizing when the Enemy is at work. You can count on him trying to steal every blessing God gives you. When God tells you something in the morning, by afternoon the Enemy will make it appear as if God's Word isn't true. He's a deceiver and he'll create illusions to undermine what God has promised. But we can learn to recognize his lies and stand against them.

It's important to remember that the Enemy cannot stop God's promises—unless we join him in unbelief and let him take them right out of our hands! So when a hiring manager tells you an offer is coming and the phone call doesn't come, stand fast in your faith. Don't jump to conclusions that the manager must have changed his mind. You may just find out that the telephone lines were out of order for a few hours so he mailed your offer instead!

Over time it will become obvious that the devil may cause delays and aggravation, but he cannot steal the blessing of the Lord when believers hold on. When you refuse to entertain fear in any form, you'll stop him in his tracks.

You shall pray according to the rules. Let's go back to Luke 11:9: *"So I say to you: Ask and it will be given to you; seek and you will find; knock and the door will be opened to you"* (NIV).

To emphasize the importance of persistence in prayer, Jesus told stories of a neighbor who needed to be roused from his sleep, and an unjust judge who needed to be pestered into doing the right thing. Unfortunately, many believers have interpreted these stories as character references for God. Let's be clear here—God isn't unjust or asleep, just as He isn't a Father who would give His children stones for bread or snakes for food!

The point of this Scripture wasn't to provide information about God but rather to reveal another important aspect of prayer—persistence. We, not God, are the ones who benefit from this aspect. We are the ones who are changed by persistent prayer.

Recall that effectual prayer includes two important components: 1) a desire based on a right motive, and 2) the belief that God will answer. The apostle John wrote, *"And this is the confidence (the assurance, the privilege of boldness) which we have in Him: [we are sure] that if we ask anything (make any request) according to His will (in agreement with His own plan), He listens to and hears us. And if (since) we [positively] know that He listens to us in whatever we ask, we also know [with settled and absolute knowledge] that we have [granted us as our present possessions] the requests made of him"* (1 John 5:14-15 AMP). Note the words, "in agreement with His own plan." Again, this is a time to be seeking God's will, not just a job.

I don't know about you, but I get impatient with my children when they keep asking for something I've already said they could have. I want them to trust that my word is good and that I'll do what I've promised. If we believe our answer is already on its way to us, would it not be silly to keep making the same request?

Still, though, Jesus tells us to keep on asking. So if we don't need to keep on reminding God about our need or pestering Him about an answer that hasn't materialized, there must be something else that calls for persistence. And here it is: We are to keep on asking about every new decision we face and every new answer we need, not the same thing over and over. Our interaction with God should become continuous so that we can pray without ceasing (see 1 Thessalonians 5:17). Job seekers need to make a habit of taking every question, every desire, and every idea to God to get His involvement with all of it, just as Jesus did.

The other reason to keep on asking can be found in Romans 10:17: *"So then faith comes by hearing and hearing by the word of God"*

(NKJV). We are to use our voice to speak the promises God has given us so that our faith in those promises will grow. Memorizing verses and reciting them aloud is another practice that seems to have fallen by the wayside these days, and that's very sad.

One of the promises we've been given about the Holy Spirit is that He *"will remind you of everything I have said to you"* (John 14:26, NIV). It is difficult to be reminded of something that we have never read or meditated upon. Our persistence, then, is rather like tending a garden. It's up to us to meditate on the Word in order to hear God's answer to our request, hide His answer in our hearts and minds and expect the fulfillment in God's perfect timing.

By the way, this is nothing like a "name it and claim it" practice where you tell God what you want Him to do for you and declare it over and over in the attempt to bring it into your life yourself. God is the One who quickens His Word to reveal His will for you. You simply receive His word and accept it by faith. I would encourage you to seek God about everything and to cast all your cares on Him because He really does care for you.

When you need a good night's sleep, ask for it saying, "Thank you, God, for Your Word that says *"When you lie down, you will not be afraid; Yes, you will lie down and your sleep will be sweet"* (Proverbs 3:24 NKJV). I ask You for sleep tonight so that I might go into my job search tomorrow refreshed."

When you're trying to get through to a hiring manager, ask for it saying: "Thank you, Father, for the promise that says *"Do you see a man who excels in his work? He will stand before kings; He will not stand before unknown men"* (Proverbs 22:29 NKJV). Please make a way for me to get through to the people You want me to speak with."

Reading God's Word out loud will not only grow your faith, it often uproots unbelief and doubts, as well. As you dwell on the promises God has given you, stay focused and ready to obey the minute you are given a direction or action to take. Just get ready to be surprised because His answers may be nothing like what you were expecting.

You shall work hard. There are two things I can confidently declare about job seekers at the start of their season of unemployment. One, they will be exhausted from apparent effort but have little to show for it, and two, they will launch out with very unrealistic expectations.

Most job seekers plan to spend 8 to 10 hours a day, every day, in search of a new position. That's not possible and it's not necessary. To hold that objective is to set yourself up for self-condemnation and failure. Think back, if you can, to the last time you started a brand new job in a completely unfamiliar organization. How productive were you on that first day when you were on your own? Most of us will admit that we weren't productive at all. We didn't know what to spend our time on, who to ask if we had questions, or how to do what we were assigned to do. We were in a very normal and completely expected learning curve. So are new job seekers.

That's why it is so important to create a realistic schedule and routine to help build your skills and your job search momentum. Think back to the discussion about managing transition. Do you recall that regaining a sense of self-worth and setting up some structure are two essential responses to effectively dealing with the first phase of transition? Well, let's leverage that information to create the perfect launch pad for your search.

Start with each one of God's five blessing objectives and ask yourself "What can I do each day to fully cooperate with this objective?" Begin with the end in mind and determine how you can arrive at the end of your job search far better off, in every area of your life, than you were when you started.

To build a relationship with God, set aside an hour at the start of your day. Spend time in His Word and in prayer to get your fuel for the day. Many job seekers keep a prayer journal to list their prayer requests, God's promises, and their prayer results as they become manifest. That's a great way to remember all that God has done.

To build a relationship with God, set aside an hour at the start of your day.

To learn to love and care for your body as a temple belonging to God, build in time to exercise, eat well and care for yourself. Make sure you are getting adequate sleep and filling your mind with positive, uplifting books, television, music and conversations.

Next, think about all the people God has placed in your life. What do you need to schedule into your day to ensure that you are building your love and relationships with them? Do you need to go to your son's ball games or your daughter's dance rehearsals? Does your spouse need time to rest and relax? Can you provide an hour of "coverage" every day to allow for that restoration? Are there letters and emails you could write, phone calls you could make or visits you could schedule to give quality time to the people you love? If so, build these things into your schedule.

Now, what projects require your attention and energy? Create project plans to clean out the garage, basement or attic. Deal with home and property repairs, gardening and closet clean-outs to find items to give away. Organize your files, file overdue tax returns and straighten out your financial situation. Now is the time! These are things that are 100% in your control and need to be accomplished, so build them into your schedule during the first four weeks of your job search. Now determine where you can volunteer. Find a place that needs your gifts and talents and give some of your time and energy away every week. Get active in your church.

Finally, schedule time for job search activities. In week one, plan on only two hours a day. Pull together your references as we discussed earlier. Then prepare your response to the question "Why are you unemployed?" Begin your self-assessment activities and initiate some Internet research to find interesting job descriptions and the related salaries for those positions in your area. If time allows, make a list of everyone you know and write down phone numbers and email addresses for each person on the list. In week two, schedule three hours a day for your job search. Prepare your CAR stories (Conditions/Actions/Results), work on your resume, continue your research and write your response to "Tell Me about Yourself."

Look for someone to help you with these activities if you need it. Find a local support group for job seekers and show up at the meetings. Contact community resources and government agencies and register, if appropriate. If Internet research won't produce the openings you need, get out and canvass your surroundings. Discover local businesses and drop in to learn about position openings.

By week three you should be able to fill four hours a day. If you've used the Job Search tips in this book and gotten connected to a job search support group or resource, you'll have a finished resume, your financial situation will be in order, your scripts will have been prepared and practiced and you should be ready to make networking calls. From this point on, your networking calls should generate activity for you to follow up on. You can also spend a few hours each week applying for advertised positions as they appear.

The bottom line is that you should schedule and spend your time as a good steward of it so that every night you'll be able to reflect on the day and feel good about it! Something important can be accomplished every day, without exception. In case you're wondering, research has shown that most job seekers spend less than fifteen hours a week on job search activities. And most of them believe they're working at it full-time. You'll be at that level in week two and will move well beyond it by the end of your first month. More importantly, you'll put yourself in a position to be a great blessing to others and to receive all that God has for you.

Don't miss this opportunity to make every moment count! You'll also reap a great reward personally as you use this structure to help you through your transition. This process will give you validation that you are still valuable and productive even though you are supposedly out of work. Just keep in mind that God's career strategy is focused on love and relationships. You're not likely to go astray if you make those your top priorities as well.

As I said before, you also need to make the commitment to be excellent at the job search process. No one is born with job search skills! They have to be learned. Far too many job seekers go into the job market without doing the work to become skilled and there's no reason for it. There are so many books, videos, seminars, support groups and Internet tips readily available. Anyone who wants to be perceived as an excellent employee should be willing to put forth the effort to be a competent job seeker as well. *"Do your best to present yourself to God as one approved, a workman who does not need to be ashamed and who correctly handles the word of truth"* (2 Timothy 2:15 NIV).

That verse reminds me of the reaction I frequently hear when I ask job seekers to practice their answers to the standard interview opener, "Tell me about yourself." Often I am told, "I hate that question . . . I NEVER know how to answer it." Really? That means these job seekers have been asked the same question time and again and they still haven't figured out how to answer it. What's wrong with that picture? If there's something you don't know how to do, or a question you don't know how to answer, you now have the time to get help and learn to do it well.

Those who want the best positions aggressively go after these unadvertised openings.

To be excellent at the job search it's also vital to realize that the vast majority of jobs are filled without advertising. These positions are found in the hidden job market. Those who want the best positions aggressively go after these unadvertised openings. The most effective job seekers make contact with every potential hiring manager to present themselves and offer their services in case a position becomes available. They learn to network, and through company employees and professional contacts, place themselves in consideration before the opening becomes public.

I told you earlier about a group of workers who had left their employer as part of an early retirement program. During one of the sessions I held with them, I gave my standard pitch about networking and the importance of letting everyone know when you're looking for a job. Just then there was a knock at the conference room door. I opened it and there stood a participant from a session a few weeks earlier. He asked if he could tell the group that what I was teaching was "really true and it worked." Well, who could resist an endorsement like that?

He told the others that he had been sitting in a donut shop one morning and happened to comment to the waitress that it felt very odd to be there in the middle of the day. She was puzzled by his comment, so he explained that he was out of work. He had never been in this donut shop in the middle of the day because he was always working. She then asked about the work he did and what kind of job he was looking for. He said that he seriously thought about just brushing the question off with a general "I'm in computers" comment but decided to practice his networking script instead.

To his great surprise, she appeared to understand the technical role he was describing and responded with "That sounds like what my brother does." She offered to put him in touch with her brother who lived and worked several states away. Again he thought about passing on the offer because it seemed a remote possibility that anything could come of it.

Nevertheless, based on my insistence about the importance of keeping every contact alive and following every opportunity to see where it might lead, he kept going. He called her brother and discovered that they both did the same type of work. In fact, it turned out that the waitress' brother was a hiring manager who wanted to fill a new regional manager position right where this candidate happened to live. You can probably guess the rest of the story. He interviewed and was hired for his perfect position. Even better, he was going to be working virtually from the comfort of his own home!

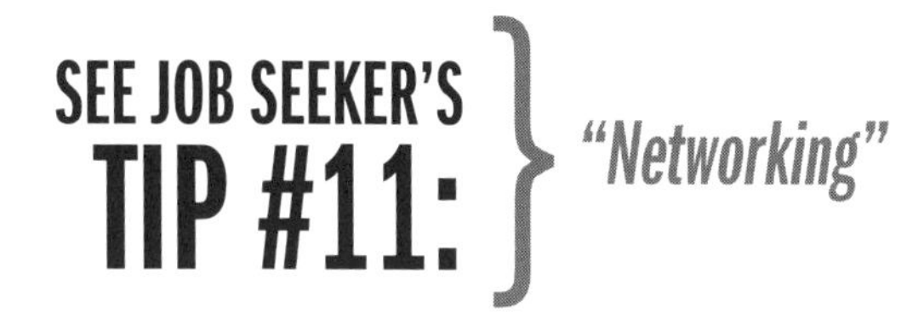

Notice how this illustrates James 2:14: *"What good is it, my brothers, if a man claims to have faith but has no deeds? Can such faith save him?"* (NIV) This man could have sincerely believed that God was going to lead him to a new job, but if he hadn't acted on his faith by making those networking connections, he would have missed this blessing. That's my point—seeking a job is hard work, but it is not impossible. All job seekers can be successful at the job search process if they'll plan their work and work their plan in accordance with Kingdom principles and the wisdom of job search best practices.

Here's a great way to measure your overall job search effectiveness. *"Be kindly affectionate to one another with brotherly love, in honor giving preference to one another; not lagging in diligence, fervent in spirit, serving the Lord; rejoicing in hope, patient in tribulation, continuing steadfastly in prayer"* (Romans 12:10-12 NKJV).

You shall let go of the past. The past will hold you prisoner if you don't let it go. Take a rubber band and stretch it over your two hands. Now try to pull your right hand forward without moving your left. At first, the rubber band will only impede your progress, but eventually, you won't be able to move at all. Your left hand will anchor the right and hold it back. If you focus on the past—people who wronged you, situations that didn't turn out as you had hoped, interviews that went badly or got cancelled—it will hold you back just like that rubber band. All of God's promises for your next assignment are in your present and in your future. There is no reason to beat yourself up over the past. Your only visits to the past should be with the guidance of the Holy Spirit for the purpose of identifying old enemy strongholds in your mind. If you still believe any of the enemy's lies about who you are, what you can do, or what you have in Christ, those mindsets need to be demolished. But as soon as that work is done, turn your attention to the road in front of you and don't look back! *"Then Jesus said to those Jews who* *believed Him, 'If you abide in My word, you are My disciples indeed. And you shall know the truth, and the truth shall make you free* (NKJV). *. . . So if the Son sets you free, you will be free indeed"* (John 8:31-32, 36 NIV).

"So if the Son sets you free, you will be free indeed."

You shall love and take no offense. Did you know that love could be a secret weapon? Check this out: *"He who dwells in the secret place of the Most High shall abide under the shadow of the Almighty. . . . He shall cover you with His feathers, And under His wings you shall take refuge; Because you have made the Lord, who is my refuge, even the Most High, your dwelling place, no evil shall befall you, nor shall any plague come near your dwelling"* (Psalm 91:1, 4, 9-10 NKJV).

I hear job seekers frequently say that they can't love certain people no matter how hard they try—people in their past, in their families, and in their circle of acquaintances. Well, no kidding. There are plenty of times when human love isn't good enough to get the job done. That's why we need God's love to pour through us. God is love. And there's a huge side benefit to this as well. When we stay close to Him, we are filled with His love. We blend right into His shadow and become invisible to the Enemy. We're under cover and hidden! Dwelling in God's loving presence seems to keep us safe and protected.

So, when you feel like you have no love to give, get with God to refill your tank. It's God's love in us that makes us selfless and other-focused, and that in itself is a great overarching career strategy. As you seek to give love and to reach out to meet the needs of others, you will walk in power and confidence. *"By this all will know that you are my disciples, if you have love for one another"* (John 13:35 NKJV). As a practical example, when you network, keep your eyes and ears open for opportunities that may help others and pass them on. Conversely, when your attention turns to yourself and your natural circumstances, the Enemy will show up right beside you to taunt you. So stay in the shadow of the Most High, and demonstrate the Kingdom by your love.

You shall give and sow seed. *"I was young and now I am old, yet I have never seen the righteous forsaken or their children begging bread. They are always generous and lend freely; their children will be blessed"* (Psalm 37:25 NIV). This has been another problematic Scripture for some job seekers. They have had to ask for help from others and they have felt like beggars. Sometimes they've received assistance they didn't even ask for, and they felt bad for accepting it. Let me offer two thoughts here. While other people are never your source, God will use others to meet your needs. It blesses them to give and it provides for you. That's a good thing all the way around. So if you're struggling with this, let go and learn to receive.

While other people are never your source, God will use others to meet your needs.

At the same time, check your own giving record. The righteous mentioned above are "always generous and lend freely." Generosity with time, talents and money is one of God's expectations for His children. No matter what our circumstances might be, we can be a blessing to others. It's another Kingdom law. *"Remember this: Whoever sows sparingly will also reap sparingly, and whoever sows generously will also reap generously"* (2 Corinthians 9:6 NIV).[12] When things get tight, continue to be generous with your money, goods, service and time. There is no need to hoard or become stingy since God has promised that His blessing will continue to flow to you. I want to make a very important point here. There is a huge difference between the prosperity God promises and the money and material wealth the world is so focused upon. God knows how to care for us and what we are able to receive and when. He knows how to provide what we need to accomplish the purposes we have been designed to accomplish. This is no get-rich-quick scheme, it's an empowerment to prosper through the work and opportunities He leads us to and its the gift of living in peace.

You shall walk by faith. *"For we walk by faith, not by sight"* (2 Corinthians 5:7 NKJV). One night a new job seeker joined our group, a bit late and quite flustered. She had just moved into the area two days earlier and had not planned on joining the group for another week. To hear her tell it, she was finishing up the dishes when she felt that she had to get to the group immediately.

It had been this woman's plan to get settled in her new home first and then start her job search in the coming week, but the urging was too strong to ignore. So she dropped what she was doing and came to church to join our group. This, by the way, is a great response to the leading of the Holy Spirit! She introduced herself to

12. This does not mean that if you give a dollar amount, a certain dollar amount will be given back to you, as the false Prosperity Gospel teaches. It simply means that the more you bless others, God will bless you, in whatever manner He chooses. Further, your giving must always be out of gratitude and obedience, never to get something in return.

the group, described the type of work she was looking for, and gave a brief overview of her administrative skills.

About ten minutes later there was a knock at the door and another newcomer joined us. This time it was a woman who introduced herself as a church member and an employer. She had an open position that she wanted to fill and thought she would share the lead with our group. As she described her job opportunity the group members began to laugh. It was the exact description given by our newest member. These two women stepped into the hall, completed an interview, and our newest member closed the deal. That night she may have set the record for the shortest job search ever! By our accounting she was officially unemployed for less than twenty minutes. That's why it pays to walk by faith and follow as the Spirit leads.

If you're new to this experience, try to remain open to the Lord's urging. *"Your ears shall hear a word behind you, saying, 'This is the way, walk in it,' Whenever you turn to the right hand Or whenever you turn to the left"* (Isaiah 30:21 NKJV). Don't expect an actual, audible voice. What you're "listening" for is a "still, small voice" a quickening in your spirit, or a sense of peace that comes with some direction or answer you've been waiting for.

You shall give thanks. Here's a Bible story to consider. David had been away in a battle. When he and his men returned, all their goods and all their family members had been stolen by the Amalekites. Needless to say, they were in deep distress, David even more so than the others, for he had lost everything. Even his men had turned against him. *"Now David was greatly distressed, for the people spoke of stoning him, because the soul of all the people was grieved, every man for his sons and his daughters. But David strengthened himself in the Lord his God"* (1 Samuel 30:6 NKJV).

There are plenty of job seekers who know this feeling! It seems to them that they've lost everything, too. In the midst of their job searches they lose the support of family and friends, and it feels like they're on their own. That's when praise and thanksgiving can be a lifesaver. *"Don't be dejected and sad, for the joy of the Lord is your strength!"* (Nehemiah 8:10).

Many of us have done this and have found that it works. You can regain your strength and joy by turning your attention to praising God for all He has already done for you. Give thanks and sing. Declare your trust in Him and keep it up. *"The Lord is my strength and my shield; my heart trusts in him, and I am helped. My heart leaps for joy and I will give thanks to him in song"* (Psalm 28:7 NIV). There are plenty of believers who have found, like King David, that help, strength and joy can be restored with a dedicated time of praise and thanksgiving.

Give thanks and sing. Declare your trust in Him and keep it up.

You shall represent the Kingdom. *"We are therefore Christ's ambassadors, as though God were making his appeal through us . . ."* (2 Corinthians 5:20 NIV). Many believers feel burdened by this thought. It's just one more performance expectation they need to meet. That's not my point in revisiting this Word. I just want to remind you that God's reputation is on the line with you.

When you make the decision to do your job search as a Kingdom citizen you gain the full backing of heaven! You can walk in confidence as a child of the King. Remember that you carry the blessing of God with you wherever you go. As surely as Laban was blessed by Jacob, and Potiphar and Pharaoh were blessed by Joseph, so will others be blessed by hiring you. That means that you can count on God to go with you and to release His favor over you.

Look for evidence of it and expect to find it. Let go of any concern that you might be misspending your energy or going to the wrong places. Because you have given your job search to the Lord, ". . . *He shall direct your paths*" (Proverbs 3:6 NKJV). This isn't a statement that He might direct you or might occasionally point out the way, but assurance that He'll stay right with you. "*The Lord directs the steps of the godly. He delights in every detail of their lives*" (Psalm 37:23).

He will keep you headed in the right direction. "*And I will give you treasures hidden in the darkness—secret riches. I will do this so you may know that I am the Lord, the God of Israel, the one who calls you by name*" (Isaiah 45:3).

I can attest to that. There were times in my search when He seemed to go ahead of me to make a way where there had been no way, to give me favor, and to keep me in confidence and peace. These are the secret riches of the Lord. So keep your eyes open for His blessings.

CHAPTER SIX

1. What are all the activities that a believer will be doing in the Seek phase of a Kingdom job search?

2. What purposes are served by the creation and use of a daily schedule during the job search?

3. What is required to be excellent at the job search process?

4. How important are love and forgiveness to the job search. Why?

JOB SEEKER'S TIP #11

Networking

How do you react when you hear the term **networking?** Do you think it's some superficial way of relating to certain people in order to get something from them? Too many job seekers think precisely that. But networking is not manipulative, nor does it take advantage of others. It's simply a quick way to get to know someone new and be known by them. The goal is to establish **a connection that will benefit both parties.** As you introduce yourself to others, be on the lookout for ways to bless them. Ask God how to pray for the people you meet and to tell you how to be a blessing to them.

How to measure your networking success:

- ***Did you make a good impression? Were you pleasant, focused and thoughtful?***
- ***Did you learn what you needed to know? (Contact's position, function and interests? Whether the organization might hire a person with your background? When and how to follow up?)***
- ***Did you get two or more new names to contact?***

Contact Guidelines

1. Identify yourself and your purpose within the first ten seconds. Explain that you are looking for a new position and would appreciate their advice.

2. Ask for three to five minutes and limit yourself to it! Be sure it's a good time for your contact to talk.

3. Briefly review your goals, special skills and work experience. Use a short version of your "Tell Me about Yourself" response.

4. Ask for information. Cover anything that may be helpful. Ask for leads to people or organizations that may have openings in your area of expertise.

5. Ask if you can use the person's name as you contact others.

6. Be positive and express confidence that something will turn up.

7. Always put your best foot forward. Do not think you can be sloppy or casual, even if you are friends with the contact.

8. Thank them for their time, and ask if you can call again.

9. Do not ask the contact to initiate calls or generate leads for you.

10. Send a follow-up email or note. Restate some key piece of information from your conversation, and express your thanks for their support and assistance.

JOB SEEKER'S TIP #12 Overcoming Objections

Most people have too much to do and too little time to do it. So realize that the objections you will likely encounter are not personal. They are most likely a by-product of hectic schedules and the effort of busy decision makers to protect their valuable time. Do not be offended, or immobilized, by objections. Just rise to the challenge and overcome the objection.

Objection: "We don't have any openings."

> **Response:** "That's all right. Right now I'm only looking for information and I understand that you are a great resource for information about the ____________ industry."

Objection: "I'm too busy right now."

> **Response:** "When could I call you back?" "Could we schedule a time to meet?" "How about a phone appointment?"

Objection: "I don't give informational interviews."

> **Response:** "I realize your time is limited. Would you have five or ten minutes right now to answer a few questions?"

Objection: "I can't help you."

Response: "I heard you were an expert in ____________. I would really value some of your insight."

Objection: "I really don't think I can help you."

Response: "Could you refer me to someone knowledgeable in the field of ________________?"

Objection: "Call Fred; he can help you."

Response: "I appreciate the referral. May I use your name?"

Objection: "I'm tied up on a project for the next few weeks."

Response: "Could you check your calendar for three weeks from today so we can schedule something? (Or "Should I call back then?")

Objection: "My workdays are already packed."

Response: "May I buy you a cup of coffee before work one morning next week to spend 15 minutes with you?"

Objection: "Send me a resume.""

Response: "Thank you. I will do that, but I would also like to meet with you at your convenience. Would you have some time next week?"

Objection: "Send your resume to Human Resources."

Response: "Is there a specific job opening in your company that you have in mind?" ("Who is the hiring manager for that position?" "May I use your name when I contact her?")

Objection: "We don't hire people with your skills."

Response: "I'm not necessarily asking about your company, but I am looking for referrals to people who may be aware of positions in __________."

Objection: "I'll call you back."

Response: "If you tell me when you will have some time, I will be happy to call you back."

CHAPTER 7

KNOCK

"And to everyone who knocks, the door will be opened."

– Matthew 7:8

Years ago, career counselors used a guideline that the average job search would generally require one month for every $10,000 of salary the job seeker hoped to earn. So a $40,000 job might take four months to find.

Now, on average, job searches at every level are taking much longer to complete. Very few searches are successfully accomplished in less than 3 months and often the process takes more than a year. As you can imagine, this is difficult news to hear.

Just completing the Seek activities—setting up a daily schedule, pulling together all the required job search materials, and practicing new interviewing and networking skills—is a challenge for most. Add to that the activities of daily living, spiritual growth and personal and volunteer projects, and it's easy to see that the seeking phase is often exhausting. It's completely understandable, then, that most job seekers hope their difficulties will end with the Seek phase and they'll graduate right into a new job. That is rarely the case, however. In fact, if we were to compare the job search to the start of a new job, the Seek phase would be Orientation, and the Knock phase would be when the real job begins. Because the job seeker is usually still uncomfortable with the whole unemployment situation and uncertain about the job search process, knocking is likely to be the most difficult phase of all. But hold on. There are ways to handle this phase successfully once you understand what to expect.

...While the length of the search may be out of the job seeker's control, the quality of the search is completely a matter of choice.

For one thing, everything in the job search will take longer than anyone—job seekers, family, friends and employers—thinks it should. Finding leads and openings online, getting through on the phone, scheduling interviews, sending out correspondence—all of it happens at a snail's pace. Most job seekers will find themselves still looking for that new job well after their anticipated deadlines. I can't tell you how often I've heard job seekers declare the date of their certain financial meltdown only to be alive and well beyond that time, although decidedly unhappy about it. But believe it or not, while the length of the search may be out of the job seeker's control, the quality of the search is completely a matter of choice.

Recently there was a single woman in our small group who was certain she would lose her house and be on the streets if she failed to secure a job in two months. As it turned out, she was in our small group, and out of work, for more than twelve months. Her car kept running (clearly by the grace of God!) and she was never hungry. In this time frame she flew all over the country to provide support for family members and friends in times of need and provided valuable support to her church and a local mission—all with no visible means of support! She also kept her home throughout this season. Eventually she put it up for sale and moved out of state. With no outside income she also managed to find a place to stay, rent a truck and make a move to a new home several states away!

When she started her job search with that supposed deadline staring her in the face, she was terrified. By the time she moved, she was smiling and at peace. Along the way she had discovered that God had assignments for her to accomplish and she needed to be out of work in order to do them. Once she had the experience of God's supernatural sustenance and gained a new focus on the Kingdom, she relocated and found her new place of employment.

The length of the job search is not the only cause of discomfort. Perhaps an even bigger one is the challenge of measuring progress. There's a tendency to believe that every day without a new job is a failed day. At the very least, job seekers feel they ought to be able to turn networking calls into interviews or interviews into offers at will. When that doesn't happen they think they're doing something wrong. The question arises, "How can job seekers know how they're doing?" Family members and friends become concerned, resources get stretched and no one seems to know how to bring the process to a close.

Still, it's not only possible, but critical, to have confidence and build faith while waiting for the new job. It is possible to approach this phase of the job search journey like that band of archaeologists we talked about in Chapter One. This is the part of the process at which the anticipated treasure is finally found! I hope you'll grant me license to create a job-search version of a fairly well-known parable to address the most common concerns that arise in this final phase of a believer's job search and to give you some encouragement to finish *"strong in the Lord and in the power of His might"* (Ephesians 6:10 NIV).

A Job Search Parable . . .

Once upon a time in a kingdom far away, a young man lost his job. Because his village was small and times were hard, there were no jobs to be found. The young man was a believer, so he immediately went to God with his situation. He asked for wisdom to know where to look for employment, and the Lord led him to Psalm 114:8: *"He turned the rock into a pool of water; yes, a spring of water flowed from solid rock."* To his surprise God told him to push the huge rock on the outskirts of town for two hours every day. This seemed an unusual assignment but the young man felt confident that he could do as God directed. Perhaps there was treasure hidden beneath the rock. Maybe a wealthy businessman would pass by and, seeing his hard work, make him a job offer. Whatever God's reason might be, the young man was determined to obey.

For two years the young man did as he was told, but the boulder never budged. The townspeople watched his futile attempts and shook their heads. There he was, day after day, rain or shine, pushing against that rock with no success. His friends started to fall away. They were embarrassed for him. Some suggested that he leave town to find work. Then, maybe he could return at a later time and buy an ox to help him move the boulder. Others insisted he had misunderstood God and that he should stop behaving like a fool. But each morning, when the young man gave thanks and prayed, he would ask God for further instruction, only to hear "keep on."

> Since the boulder-pushing assignment required only two hours a day, the young man was able to fill his remaining hours with many acts of service and productive activities. He made gifts in his wood shop for the village children and visited with the village elders. He sang in the choir and helped with the church landscaping. He told everyone he met that he was looking for employment and followed up on every lead he was given, to no avail. He helped neighbors with chores and repairs. They, in return, provided him with meals and supplies, and so his needs were met. Every day for two full years he did whatever he could find to do, and every night he fell asleep with a clear conscience. His only frustration was that boulder. Though he daily grew in strength, he could not make it budge.
>
> Then one day the King showed up in the village, unexpected and unannounced. He had heard of the young man and had come to meet him. The young man was greatly embarrassed. "I am sorry you made the trip," said the youth, "for I have failed at what God called me to do. The boulder is right where it was at the start. I have not moved it an inch,"
>
> "That's not how I see it," replied the King. "You see, moving the rock was never God's purpose. You just didn't know that for the past two years I have been praying that God would give me a commander for my army. He sent me to you today, and now I understand why. You continued faithfully in this effort, without reward or any sign of accomplishment. No matter what, you never quit. Your obedience to God's instruction was the very preparation that proves you are the strong, trustworthy and faithful man I need as the leader of my army. As of today you are in command."

This story helps to answer the following common job-seeker questions. I'm sure you see the not-so-subtle points I want to make.

What does God really expect of me while I'm out of work?

Let's see how God has answered this question. "*. . . The Lord has told you what is good and this is what he requires of you: to do what is right, to love mercy, and to walk humbly with your God"* (Micah 6:8).

The young man in this parable made a great strategic decision when he went immediately to God with his situation. He chose to walk humbly with God by accepting his initial assignment and meeting with God in prayer every morning for further direction. Beyond that, he obeyed without question. Even though he didn't understand the purpose for pushing the boulder, he did as he was told and kept on doing it. Obedience requires perseverance. Until we get a different command, we are to continue as instructed. It's not up to us to determine when enough is enough.

From what I've observed across the years, God gives the commands, manages the timing and brings the outcome. It is our responsibility to do the assignment with excellence until God brings the victory. *"The horse is prepared for the day of battle, but the victory belongs to the Lord" (*Proverbs 21:31). Humility with the Lord is the result of our complete agreement that He will call the shots and we will follow His lead, no matter what. Notice also that the young man didn't make his unemployed self the center of attention. He took full advantage of his available time to make a Kingdom difference in the lives of those around him. With no special instruction to do it, he acted in love and mercy. He simply set out daily to give his talents away and share the love of God.

The third thing God requires is that we do what is right. When it comes to the job search process, this really isn't a mystery. There are right ways to do a job search and there are wrong ways. That's why the Seek phase is so important. This is when job seekers learn and master the best practices of the process—self assessment, preparation, resume writing, networking and interview skills, for example. Because we know that God also wants us to receive all five of his job search blessings, believers need to do the things that position them to receive those gifts as well. Following a daily routine that includes self-care, personal and volunteer projects, giving, attention to relationships, having fellowship with God and performing job search activities is the believer's "right thing" to do. So this question can be answered with the guideline, "**knock and obey**."

When will this end and what can I do to speed it up?

As you can see, this question is closely related to the first. The answer is only God knows, but your obedience and faith are clearly important factors. If you accept that God is your employer and that He has given you assignments to accomplish, it's not likely He'll give you new work until you've completed what He's already assigned. The young man in our story understood this. He didn't stop what he was doing to find a better or more reasonable assignment. But many job seekers do precisely that. Job seekers often come into the group convinced that God wants them to go on a mission trip or do some personal project, but they decide not to do it until they have a job and the money they need.

I just read about a man who lost his job, and despite thinking that he was being foolish and that the timing wasn't right, he went on a mission trip to Africa. To his great surprise, God used that trip to set him up in his own business. Now he is in the business of selling and distributing handmade beads and baskets, employing women in Africa, and supporting their families as well as his own with the new enterprise. While your unquestioning obedience and close, continual contact with God may keep you from delaying your job search process, I don't think there's anything you can do to accelerate it and that's actually a good thing. Remember, God stands outside of time and has a perfect view of the future. He is orchestrating all the variables to ensure that we are developed and positioned in line with His perfect will. Why would we, in our impatience, want to interfere with that? So here's my advice, stay focused on God and others, and you'll be far less concerned with the length of the job search process. Leave the timing up to God and trust the promise: *"At the right time, I, the Lord, will make it happen"* (Isaiah 60:22). So, if you want to make this journey as quickly as possible, **knock and trust God**.

How do I know I am hearing from God?

Or perhaps you've asked the question this way: "Is it God, is it me, or is it the Enemy that I'm hearing?" I remember when I was first learning to listen for the voice of God. I thought I was to ask my question and sit quietly for as long as I could until I heard something deep and spiritual. That technique might work for some people, but it definitely didn't work for me. I think this must be an experience shared by many, because quite a few job seekers complain that they don't hear from God.

Consider, though, that God doesn't need to speak personally about everything because His Word already has many of our answers. For many believers, the experience of unemployment is the time when stewardship finally gets the attention it deserves. God's Word has much to say about the economy of God and the behaviors that enable us to withstand the storms of life. Now is the time to learn those principles and put them into practice. To understand the character of God, His instructions for us and His will in many situations, we just have to read His Word with purpose and intensity. *"All Scripture is given by inspiration of God, and is profitable for doctrine, for reproof, for correction, for instruction in righteousness, that the man of God may be complete, thoroughly equipped for every good work"* (2 Timothy 3:16-17).

God's Word is alive and it will sometimes "speak" directly and personally to your situation. God will draw your attention to some verse and provide the revelation that shows how it applies to your situation, just as if He were talking directly to you. Other times, the Holy Spirit in you will bring scriptures to your remembrance that will guide you in the way to go. At other times God will speak through others and we'll experience a peace and understanding that what we are hearing is the answer to our prayer. These are just some of the many ways we can "hear" the voice of God. Our part is to earnestly seek Him and He promises that He will be found.

Receiving a word from God is a very different experience than the way our minds race when trying to figure out the answer to a problem.

When the answer we come up with only seems to be the lesser of all evils or the path of least resistance, most likely that answer is our own invention. God's answers are often so brilliant and suddenly obvious that we don't understand how we could have missed coming up with them ourselves! Then again, it's not unusual for God's direction to make no "sense" to us at all. Look at the parable again. It isn't likely the young man dreamed up the idea of pushing on that boulder. It certainly made no sense as a job search strategy. Nor would fear drive a person to take up boulder pushing as the way to find work.

There is an inner conviction that comes by consistently reading God's Word and seeking to understand His will and His character. From this practice and regular times of prayer we come to know that God's voice is unmistakable and well worth waiting for. Jesus tells us that He is the Good Shepherd and His sheep know His voice. This needs to become a top priority in our lives—to recognize His voice. Of course, as soon as you hear it, take action. The young man of our story understood that his future was going to flow from that rock, so he stayed with it. Don't let anyone or anything talk you out of what the Lord tells you. Just **knock with confidence**.

What do I do when God is silent?

This is a big concern—and a common experience—for believers and job seekers alike. Apparently, it's also a necessary part of our faith development. When God is silent, we have to make a decision to continue to trust or to abandon our faith and go off on our own.

When he faced God's silence, the young man in our parable remained as fixed as the boulder he was trying to move. The best advice is just what the young man heard in his heart—keep on doing what you were last told to do. Don't quit and don't waver. *"Let your roots grow down into him, and let your lives be built on him. Then your faith will grow strong in the truth you were taught, and you will overflow with thankfulness"* (Colossians 2:7).

Job made his decision on this issue too: *"Though He slay me, yet will I trust Him"* (Job 13:15 NKJV). Job knew where he stood in his faith, and he didn't budge an inch when God was silent. So even in the silence, **knock and keep knocking**.

How do I know if I'm making progress?

What does success look like? This goes right along with the question, "What do I say to the people, including my spouse, who think I'm doing the wrong things, or doing things wrong?"

This constant question also begs us to look again at the parable of the young man. He thought his progress was going to be measured by the movement of the boulder. But moving the boulder was not his assignment. He was told to push the boulder, not move it. Job seekers aren't responsible for outcomes either. The measure of a networking call is not a resulting job opening or an invitation to an interview (although those are certainly nice when they happen!).

A great networking call is measured by three things—creation of a positive first impression, information gathered about the contacts and their workplaces, and the acquisition of two more names to call. A successful interview is one where the job seeker has a solid CAR story for every question asked and the interviewer is left with a strong sense of trust in the job seeker.

The key to successful networking is "uncensored calling." Job seekers aren't to pick and choose whom to call based on the likelihood of a successful outcome. The command is *"Knock and the door will be opened,"* not, "Decide where you want to knock based on your idea of which door will most likely open"!

The key to successful networking is "uncensored calling."

There are measures of excellence like this for every activity, and these are what set the standards that indicate progress. When I began my job as an executive recruiter, I was trained for a few days in the essentials of making calls to potential employers and the process for finding and developing job orders. Then came the day when I was to make those phone calls on my own. I was told that if I made 30 calls a day, I would be successful.

Armed with that knowledge, I began my day. In short order more than 30 hiring managers flat-out rejected me. I kept calling and throughout the afternoon another 40 hung up on me as well. In one day I had tallied up 70 failures. Convinced that I was in the wrong job, I went to my manager prepared to resign. I explained what I had done and that I was obviously not cut out for executive recruiting.

To my surprise my manager burst into laughter. He told me that 70 rejections in one day was an all-time high! He then declared that anyone who would keep calling after 30 rejections was definitely destined for success. I didn't find my 70-rejection milestone a particularly comforting record to hold, but nonetheless he assured me that if I would keep at it, success would follow. I didn't really believe him, but I was determined to follow my instructions to the letter, just to prove I couldn't succeed. To my utter surprise I didn't fail. I became the rookie of the year for that office!

So, when you meet with skepticism and criticism (and you will!) you need to gauge your success accurately. A growing network to call, completed projects, deepening faith and a trail of blessings and service to others are the true measures of progress. The rest is up to God.

I want to remind you again of the great promise found in Isaiah 40:31: *"But those who trust in the Lord will find new strength. They will soar high on wings like eagles. They will run and not grow weary. They will walk and not faint."* You too can **knock and faint not**.

How do I know if my faith is working?

Put another way, how much faith do I need? What was the indicator of the young man's faith in the parable? It was nothing more than his continued activity in obedience to his instructions. He continued to push that boulder because he had faith that God would do something as a result of his effort. *"Now faith is the substance of things hoped for, the evidence of things not seen"* (Hebrews 11:1 NKJV). The New Living Translation puts it this way, *"Faith is the confidence that what we hope for will actually happen; it gives us assurance about things we cannot see."*

It's not unusual for job seekers to become discouraged and to question if their faith is working. Let's look at three common problems that might undermine confidence and what to do about them.

1. You aren't **seeing** any "results." I have a garden, and when I plant something I put a little cardboard sign in the spot to remind me of what I planted. That little sign is my "title deed" for the harvest. Until my tomatoes come in, that sign with the tomatoes pictured on it stands there to assure me of my harvest. Faith in God is our "title deed." And, we don't need great faith or strong faith to receive from Him. In Luke 17:5-6, the Apostles were concerned about their faith too and asked Jesus to increase their faith. Do you remember what He told them? If their faith was only as big as a mustard seed, they could uproot trees with their voices alone.

   Now, don't go thinking that if you can't literally transplant Sequoias with your vocal chords something is wrong. Jesus' point is that the object of your faith is what's important—Almighty God—not the "quantity" of your faith. If you've never tested your faith before, start small. Ask God for fresh ideas and praise Him when they come. Ask for the energy to complete a project or insights about your gifts and talents. As you see God fulfill your needs according to His will, your faith will grow, just like that tiny mustard seed, until you are able to wait patiently and confidently even when God's answer is a long time in coming. A tiny bit of true faith, grounded in submissiveness to the will of God, is all that is necessary. So, rather than worry about the quantity of your faith, turn your attention to the development of patience. *"Be joyful in hope, patient in affliction, faithful in prayer"* (Romans 12:12 NIV).

2. You aren't **taking action** until you see some results. Okay, here we'll find that the problem may not be in your faith or in God's answers. It may be in the failure to follow directions. Faith won't work if you don't! His Word won't produce results in your job search if you won't make contacts, volunteer your talents, spend time in prayer, and practice your job search skills. *"For as the body without the spirit is dead, so faith without works is dead also"* (James 2:26 NKJV). You have to step out in faith and do things trusting in the wisdom of others and the Word of God before you will be able to prove for yourself that faith works.

3. You aren't seeing **the results you asked for**. This is a really big issue but it isn't a sign of insufficient faith. You see there's a big difference between "standing in faith" and wishful thinking. It isn't up to us to pick and choose what we would like in any given situation and then to declare that we are "standing in faith" for it.

   I frequently hear job seekers declare that they are standing in faith for a specific job or opportunity but there is no basis for their confidence. God didn't reveal that this was the opportunity He was providing . . . they just assumed that they could persuade God to give it if they claimed it "in faith." That belief is based on an error that has crept into the church, and it's causing a great deal of pain and disillusionment. Scriptures tell us that we are to listen for His voice, receive His instructions and then cling, in faith, to what we're told personally.

   As confirmation and validation, we need to study the Word so we will know that what we're "hearing" lines up with the principles of God's economy. The Holy Spirit is our Guide and Teacher in this. Just know that God will give you the answer you need in His perfect time and nearly always it will be better than the answer you envisioned. Don't listen to anyone who tells you this works the other way around and that believers get to tell God what to do and when!

In other words, don't try to use your faith to do God's part. Faith has been given to us so that we can stay in peace and expectancy as God works. Faith is not the power to manifest the outcomes we want. Trust me, faith in God works just as it is supposed to once we rightly understand it, so stop telling God how big your problems are compared to your little faith and start telling your problems how big your faith in God is. With the help of the Holy Spirit, **knock and grow in faith**.

What can I do to keep from losing heart?

What many job seekers are really saying with this question is, "I just want to quit." Oh no, you don't! You're in the home stretch now. Unfortunately the job search isn't neatly organized into laps, or innings or quarters, so you can't tell how close you are to the finish. But don't break before you break through! The pressure you're feeling could just be an Enemy attack.

The closer you get to the goal, the more you're likely to see the Enemy's attempts to block you from crossing that finish line. Just bear in mind that he has no real power. He cannot enter into your situation unless you open the door to fear. All he can do is work on your thoughts to get you to turn around, go in circles or sit down.

Neither can you let your guard down if things are going well. If you've ever overcome an addiction or sinful behavior, you can rest assured that the Enemy will pull out a fall-back strategy to see if he can entice you back into the snares of the past. *"If you think you are standing strong, be careful not to fall. The temptations in your life are no different from what others experience. And God is faithful. He will not allow the temptation to be more than you can stand. When you are tempted, he will show you a way out so that you can endure"* (1 Corinthians 10:12-13). If temptation doesn't work, the Enemy may try a different tactic, the three-part attack: Distraction, Delay and Discouragement.

SEE JOB SEEKER'S TIP #13: *"Getting Through"*

The toughest blows will sometimes come through the words of those who matter the most to you. If this happens to you, don't take it personally and don't get angry or offended. Walk in love and keep your faith. The believer's best strategy is to stay focused on the instructions of God:

> *"For this very reason, make every effort to add to your faith goodness; and to goodness, knowledge; and to knowledge, self-control; and to self-control, perseverance; and to perseverance, godliness; and to godliness, brotherly kindness; and to brotherly kindness, love. For if you possess these qualities in increasing measure, they will keep you from being ineffective and unproductive in your knowledge of our Lord Jesus Christ"* (2 Peter 1:5-8 NIV).

Family members will usually settle down when they sec you praying and testifying to the goodness of God. When your faith is firm, they will be able to draw strength from you. It's when you are shaky that they panic. *"This is my command—be strong and courageous! Do not be afraid or discouraged. For the Lord your God is with you wherever you go"* (Joshua 1:9).

Prayer, Praise and the Word of God will keep you strong no matter how long it takes to prevail. Nothing will stop the promise of Luke 11:9 and Matthew 7:7, *"Keep on knocking, and the door will be opened to you."*

One final note on this topic: Be especially vigilant when you receive your job offer, land that new account or open your business. Don't be surprised if the Enemy takes one last shot right when you think your victory is sure. *"Do not be afraid of sudden terror, nor of trouble from the wicked when it comes; for the Lord will be your confidence, and will keep your foot from being caught"* (Proverbs 3:25-26 NKJV).

No matter how things look, put your trust in the Lord, obey His Word, and refuse to be moved. *"Therefore do not cast away your confidence, which has great reward. For you have need of endurance, so that after you have done the will of God, you may receive the promise"* (Hebrews 10:35-36 NKJV). You have everything it takes to **knock and overcome**.

How do I handle the embarrassment of being unemployed this long?

The answer to this one might really surprise you. Do you remember that you work for the Lord? He might be building your strength like He did for the young man in our parable. He might be getting other people and circumstances into place—we don't know what He's up to. But whatever God is doing, dealing with your embarrassment is not His assignment, it's yours. So let it go.

Make the move from embarrassed to ambassador! This is a perfect time to let others in on the Source of your confidence and peace. *"And if someone asks about your Christian hope, always be ready to explain it"* (1 Peter 3:15).

Even before you land your next job you can witness for the Lord. You know God is good and you know He will provide. *"And God is able to make all grace abound to you, so that in all things at all times, having all that you need, you will abound in every good work"* (2 Corinthians 9:8 NIV).

If you find you can't witness with integrity and boldness, spend more time with the Lord in prayer. Go back into the Word and learn about Him to build your faith until you can wholly trust Him. Then declare aloud, and every chance you get, that God's Word is true and unemployment or misemployment will not stop Him from blessing those who believe in and obey Him. You can be assured that you will draw a great deal of attention when you take this stand. You may be the butt of jokes, just like the young man in my parable, and some will probably try to convince you that your faith is misplaced. You know that it is not.

> *"We give great honor to those who endure under suffering. For instance, you know about Job, a man of great endurance. You can see how the Lord was kind to him at the end, for the Lord is full of tenderness and mercy" (James 5:11).*

It is up to believers to get this word out. *"But how can they call on him to save them unless they believe in him? And how can they believe in him if they have never heard about him? And how can they hear about him unless someone tells them?"* (Romans 10:14). We can't wait until the job search is over, because no one will be watching then. This is your big chance to **knock and witness for the Kingdom**.

How will I make ends meet?

Did you see what happened to the young man in the story? He took his eyes off his natural circumstances and focused on giving to others and—most importantly—he kept giving God thanks. All his needs were met while he was working on other things. I've seen this countless times and I've lived it. Somehow food is stretched, cars keep going, resources come, and life goes on. The key lies in thanks and in giving.

When I was a single mom I had a "Thanksgiving dinner" whenever my situation appeared impossible. My children and I would eat a couple of turkey drumsticks and all the fixings and give thanks to God for taking care of us. Actually, my plan backfired a bit, because after a few of these dinners, my kids would ask, "What's wrong?" every time they smelled turkey! We had turkey so often in those years that neither of them will eat turkey today. Nevertheless, God got us through every trial, and we came to trust that He always would.

Finally, as we learned in the Seek phase, we can give too, no matter what our circumstances. *"Give, and it will be given to you: good measure, pressed down, shaken together, and running over will be put into your bosom. For with the same measure that you use, it will be measured back to you"* (Luke 6:38 NKJV).

Everyone has something to give, beyond the tithe. It brings such joy to forget ourselves and reach out to meet the needs of others. When you start to feel needy yourself, try this and see if the act of giving doesn't make you feel blessed to be able to do it. Most importantly, give whenever God directs you to give because this is often His way of bringing you an answer to your prayers. This doesn't always have to be money. You can be generous with your time and talents, as well. The last bit of meal and oil that the widow gave to the prophet was all it took to sustain her through the next three years of famine. God hasn't changed; what He did in response to her prayers, trust and willingness to give in obedience, He will do for every job seeker, so **knock and keep giving**.

I know there are some of you who may be unconvinced by what I've shared. Perhaps you think my parable was farfetched. Let me close with this amazing true-life example that occurred in my small group ministry.

A man showed up one night and instantly caught the vision of the Kingdom job search process. He got so excited about it that he immediately volunteered to become an assistant group leader. He taught the principles I've given you and he lived them. He loved the idea that he was working for God and enthusiastically volunteered his time in the youth ministry and as an usher at every service. He actively worked to find and share leads with others in the group, determined to get seed in the ground for his harvest.

Quite a few group members found their next jobs from the connections he provided. He spent time in the Word and appeared to follow every direction he was given. Surprisingly, nothing opened up for him. His wife went back to work and quickly received a promotion, but he remained on the sidelines. He networked and he interviewed, but week after week he came up empty. This went on for two full years! His family was provided for and he was a great blessing to others, but he remained unemployed. I thought he was going to set a new unemployment world record.

Then one morning he called to say that he had just been invited to interview in the place he most wanted to work. He was a chemist and this position was in the university laboratory where he had worked as an intern years earlier. He was excited and so was I. We prayed that God's will would be done during the interview, and the man agreed to call with a report as soon as the interview ended. As promised, he called but only to say he was completely baffled by what he had experienced. The manager had not interviewed him but rather had walked him around to introduce him to all his new coworkers. He even showed him a desk and said, "Here's your desk." He was never asked a single question the whole time he was there! The manager simply sent him home with the promise that he'd get a call in the afternoon.

He asked if I thought he should accept the anticipated job offer on the spot or think about it for a while, not wanting to appear too eager. My advice was to pray about the salary he would need and, if that amount was offered, to accept it immediately. Forget game-playing. It was time for him to get back into the workplace! That afternoon he did indeed receive an offer for the exact amount he wanted and he accepted immediately.

The final chapter of this story came the next day. Apparently, two hours after he had received and accepted his job offer, a call came into the Human Resources office telling them that a hiring freeze had just been put in place. They were to extend no offers of employment and recall all offers that were still outstanding. The staffing manager explained that his offer had already been accepted so it couldn't be recalled. Approval was granted for him to start in his new position as planned. God's window of opportunity had opened just long enough to get him in the door!

SEE JOB SEEKER'S TIP #16: "Do You Have Any Questions?"

Perhaps this "Job Seeker's Psalm" will serve to remind you of these truths as you walk through the most challenging phase of your job search. My advice to you is to keep your eyes on the prize. Guard your heart above all else, for it determines the course of your life (see Proverbs 4:23).

Let me offer this from God's Word: *"So let's not get tired of doing what is good. At just the right time we will reap a harvest of blessing if we don't give up"* (Galatians 6:9). **Knock and be encouraged**.

THE JOB SEEKER'S PSALM

The Lord is my Employer; I shall never be out of work.
He makes me to be His representative. He leads me to
places where I can be a blessing.
He restores my confidence.

He leads me in and out of assignments for my soul's sake.
And even though I walk through a season of
unemployment, I will fear no evil,
for You are with me.

Your Word and Your Spirit, they empower me. You
prepare a new job before me in the presence of my critics
and doubters. You anoint my actions with favor.
My days are filled with Your provisions.

Surely peace and productivity will follow me all the days
of my search, and I will reenter the workplace, with You,
at the perfect time.

CHAPTER SEVEN

1. What does God expect of a Kingdom job seeker? Discuss all three requirements and how they apply to job seekers.

2. How can we recognize the voice of God and know it is He who is speaking?

3. How should job seekers measure their progress to determine if they're doing the right things well?

4. What determines a believer's level of faith, and how can great faith be developed?

JOB SEEKER'S TIP #13 Getting Through

IDENTIFY THE RIGHT PERSON

- Call the main phone number and ask the receptionist for the name of the executive of the function you are targeting. "Could you please tell me the name of the Vice President of R&D?"

- If the receptionist is unwilling to give you this information, ask to be transferred to the department's administrative assistant.

- If you hit another brick wall with the AA, call the main number and ask for Accounts Payable or Billing. When they answer, explain that you would like to reach the "Director of _______________." Ask if they could give you that person's name and extension to prevent any further confusion and misplaced calls like this one!

- Whenever you are given a name and title, ask the company representative to confirm it. "I have some correspondence for Fred Ramirez. Is he still the Vice President of Sales?" Confirm spelling, title, and address.

- If the name you get is initials, an unfamiliar name or a unisex first name, ask, "Is this a man or woman?" You don't want to get that wrong!

SPEAK TO THE RIGHT PERSON

If you find yourself getting blocked by telephone handlers, review these tips.

- Use a tone of voice that sounds professional and encourages help. Don't sound demanding.

- Be brief. Be patient. Be courteous.

- Get the name of every administrative assistant and telephone answerer. It is much more cordial and effective to address someone by name, especially when calling repeatedly.

- Ask for the targeted individual by name. "Is (first name) in today?" is a good way to determine if you'll need to delay calling for another day.

USE THE RIGHT APPROACH

If you encounter interference and can't get to the person you are trying to reach, try the following.

- Ask God for angelic support and Holy Spirit guidance. Follow as the Spirit leads.

- Find a bridge to the decision maker. "This is Sara Chang. Is Steve available? Joe Washington asked me to call him." Mentioning the name of the person who referred you is one of the most effective means of overcoming interference. It's why you ask networking contacts if you can use their names!

- Establish a relationship with the administrative assistant and ask for help.

- Call at off-hours (such as early morning, during the secretary's lunch break, or after hours) when the targeted individual may pick up the phone personally.

- Leave a voice mail message if you keep getting blocked by the administrative assistant.

- Call more than four times. In my experience, most job seekers quit at three calls, never realizing that the AA just might stop blocking the calls if they persist in calling a few more times. I can't tell you the number of times my Admin became a job seeker's advocate and asked me to speak with the person when it became apparent that the caller wasn't going to quit.

JOB SEEKER'S TIP #14 Illegal Questions

Employers sometimes ask illegal questions during an interview. Most won't even know they're doing anything wrong. As you go through your job search, you're likely to discover the hard way that very few hiring managers have been trained in interviewing. So don't get offended if they ask something inappropriate or personal. Try to figure out what they're really concerned about and answer that hidden question.

On the other hand—if your discernment tells you there is a wrong motive behind the question, answer the question politely but consider long and hard if you want to work in that environment.

What's the real concern when they ask these questions?

Actual Question: Can you handle the pressure and fatigue of this kind of job at your age?

> **Likely Concern:** Are you still committed to working or do you want to coast for the rest of your career?
>
> **Answer:** "My track record indicates that I consistently do whatever it takes to get the job done right. I am committed to doing excellent work."

Actual Questions: How is your health? Are you handicapped in any way?

Likely Concerns: Are you dependable? Is your attendance good? Will you cause us any headaches?

Answer: "My past experience can attest to my dependability, and I will be happy to take a pre-employment examination at your request."

Actual Questions: Do you have children? Do you plan to have children?

Likely Concern: Will you be focused on your work or distracted?

Answer: "I am committed to my career and to providing real value to my employer. My family situation will not interfere with that."

Actual Question: Do you own your own home?

Likely Concern: Are you stable?

Answer: "Are you concerned about my stability? My prior work history indicates that I am."

JOB SEEKER'S TIP #15

"What Salary Are You Looking For?"

Talk about a question that strikes fear in the hearts of most job seekers—this one would have to be at the top of the list! I think that's because most candidates think this is really asking, "What are you worth?" Additionally, they fear that their entire compensation future hangs on their answer. Let's see if we can banish that fear and provide an effective response to this common interview question.

KEY CONCEPT #1: The salary paid for a job is determined by the job, not by the person who holds the job. The salary offered is **not a reflection of your personal worth.**

KEY CONCEPT #2: If you will be performing work directly related to your skills and past experience, your salary should be comparable to or higher than that of your prior position. Salary is a good way to determine if the position is appropriate for you. A step backwards in salary should only occur with a difference in cost of living or a change to a new field or line of work.

HOW WILL YOU KNOW THE APPROPRIATE SALARY RANGE?

1. **Research similar positions** to determine the market value (Salary.com).

2. **Determine how well you match** the position require-

ments—are you a long shot or trainee for this type of work, an absolute expert or someone in between?

3. **Know what you require financially.**

4. **Determine your trade-offs.** If the potential salary is less than desirable, what other factors would have to be in place to make you willing to work there?

POSITIVE RESPONSES TO THE QUESTIONS:

1. **What salary are you looking for?** "My market research indicated . . ."

2. **What are you worth?** Smile, then say, "You couldn't afford that! Let's just talk about your pay for the position."

3. **What will it take to bring you on board?** Give a truthful answer based on your current financial needs and your market research.

NEGOTIATE ONLY WHEN ONE OR MORE OF THE FOLLOWING APPLY:

- ***The position is executive level or requires unique and hard-to-find skills and abilities.***
- ***The position can significantly impact company earnings and you have the experience to make that impact.***
- ***The most desirable candidate has other offers pending.***
- ***The position has been vacant for a long time and there's a strong need to get it filled quickly.***
- ***There are absolutely no other candidates in contention for the position and you know this for a fact.***

JOB SEEKER'S TIP #16

"Do You Have Any Questions?"

Here it is—the question that generally signals the close of the interview. Most candidates breathe a sigh of relief when they hear it, and they blow the question off with "No, not at this time" or "Not really."

What they don't realize is that they've just been handed the perfect opportunity to make a powerful and lasting impression. You've heard the phrase "leaving a good taste in the mouth"? Use this question to end strong!

DON'T—

- ***Ask about salary or benefits***
- ***Ask what the specific duties of the position will be***
- ***Start talking about how much you'd like (or need) the job***
- ***Say "No, no questions."***

DO—

- ***Ask, "How do I fit?" or "Do you think my qualifications match what you're looking for?"***
- ***Ask, "What concerns do you have about my ability to do this position?"***

- ***Ask, "What is the best way for me to follow up on this? What are the next steps in your process?"***

LISTEN CAREFULLY TO THE INTERVIEWER'S FEEDBACK.

Many will simply tell you that you are a good candidate for the position but they have other candidates to consider and they'll get back to you. Occasionally, an interviewer will express an actual concern. When they do, use the following three steps to address the issue:

1. **Express understanding and agreement.** "I understand that my lack of ________________ experience might be a concern for you."

2. **Offer a compensating factor.** "I have taken other positions like the one at XYZ company that we discussed earlier without possessing all the required skills. I was able to learn _____________ on the job while delivering results."

3. **Express your interest.** "I just want you to know that I am very interested in this position and I believe my ______________________________, __________________, and __________________ skills could really make a good contribution in this position."

CHAPTER 8

COMMENCEMENT

"You are the light of the world—like a city on a hilltop that cannot be hidden. No one lights a lamp and then puts it under a basket. Instead, a lamp is placed on a stand, where it gives light to everyone in the house. In the same way, let your good deeds shine out for all to see, so that everyone will praise your heavenly Father."

– Matthew 5:14-16

Years ago I became concerned about the chaos that seems to be growing everywhere in society. I wanted to know the cause, so in prayer I asked God if He was behind it or if it was the work of the Enemy. The answer I received was simply, "Yes."

In my mind, I saw a vision of choppy, dark water filled with people who were attempting to keep their heads above the waves. The people were terrified and they were crying out for help. I could see them looking around for some form of rescue.

Then I saw anchored channel markers giving off light. The markers were actually people too. But these people were calm and at peace. They stood above the waves, on the water's surface. Soon, those in the water spotted these human beacons of light and began to reach for them and swim toward them.

I realized that the people with the light were believers that God had established to guide the way in the midst of chaos. They were anchored and established in His love and peace, and they held the answers for the hurting world. I saw the words of Genesis 1:1-3: *"In the beginning God created the heavens and the earth. The earth was formless and empty, and darkness covered the deep waters. And the Spirit of God was hovering over the surface of the waters. Then God said, 'Let there be light,' and there was light."*

I understood that God is allowing the chaos and darkness to grow. All the decisions that are made on a daily basis, contrary to His love and His Kingdom, are increasing the darkness and fueling the chaos. And God is watching and moving.

In the darkness He is positioning His children to shine with His glory. The darkness we are witnessing right now may be the plan of our Enemy who still believes that he is winning the battle against God. He uses the cover of darkness and this time of confusion to bring destruction and pain. So once again much of our world appears dark and chaotic. But God is right here hovering over His creation to redeem it. And once again He sends light—the light of His Kingdom in the form of His disciples and ambassadors.

There's a reason that I said "disciples" and not "believers." It's because countless believers are not anchored or established in peace. They don't have the deep, personal relationship with Christ that banishes every form of fear from their lives. In the chaos, these believers are struggling in the waters along with a multitude of the lost. How has this happened?

I'm convinced that these believers have never experienced the winning, one-two combination of a life crisis paired with the overcoming response of God. They didn't get to practice and build their faith in Him by seeing His response to a serious, real life challenge.

They may have lost their jobs, but no one taught them a Kingdom response to their circumstances. Perhaps they encountered difficulties and were told that the conditions were God's will for them so they never went to Him for help to overcome the problems. How many of us were taught "God will never give you more sorrow than you can bear"? What are believers going to do with the conflict that is created when they hear that their loving heavenly Father is also the cause of their sorrows?

If we look to Jesus as the One who reveals the Father to us, we see Him calming storms, not creating them, healing, not afflicting, and replacing sorrow with joy. Here's what He said about His purpose on Earth:

> *"For I have come down from heaven, not to do My own will, but the will of Him who sent Me"* (John 6:38 NKJV).

> *"I have come that they may have life, and that they may have it more abundantly"* (John 10:10 NKJV).

> *"I have come as a light into the world, that whoever believes in Me should not abide in darkness"* (John 12:46 NKJV).

Now it is up to us to share the good news of Jesus Christ and to let other job seekers know that God is ready to lead them through the process just as He has lead and supported you. If you've worked your way through this book as a believer and Kingdom job seeker, then I am confident that you have been changed in some significant ways, whether you realize it yet or not.

This means you are now ready for the next phase of this faith journey—commencement. You have your personal job search testimony and a Kingdom responsibility to spread the word. You could have been left to struggle in the darkness, too. *"But you are not like that, for you are a chosen people. You are royal priests, a holy nation, God's very own possession. As a result, you can show others the goodness of God, for he called you out of the darkness into his wonderful light"* (1 Peter 2:9).

You have been given a new understanding of God's involvement in the workplace that emboldens believers to venture forth into a job search or career transition without fear. You are now someone who can help other believers discover God's will for them in the workplace. There's nothing to fear because the world belongs to and remains under the authority of Jesus Christ, our true Employer.

...The world belongs to and remains under the authority of Jesus Christ, our true Employer.

Yes, there is an apparent usurper on the earthly throne right now, but he is powerless against the will of God. All that he does is based on the deception that he is strong and powerful and cannot be overcome. You and I know better, for *"... He who is in you is greater than he who is in the world"* (1 John 4:4 NKJV). We are that city set on a hill, shining so brightly that it cannot be missed. Even now, Kingdom job seekers attract attention with amazing testimonies of things that happen in their journeys. We are called to tell others of the goodness of God and His plan for their victory. In the same way, *"let your good deeds shine out for all to see, so that everyone will praise your heavenly Father"* (Matthew 5:16).

I hope that by now you understand that your ultimate victory will be a Kingdom victory. From the start of this book and all the way through it we've talked about the battle that is raging between the forces of a fallen world and the Kingdom of our God. You learned early that you were engaged in this battle whether you wanted to be or not. We even found out that you and I were destined to be officers in this battle for the workplace because we are directly related to the King!

So it should come as no surprise to find out that your responsibility doesn't end when you land in a new place of employment. There's a ministry for you now in the workplace. You're one of those channel markers that others will reach for, and God has equipped you to point them to safety in Christ. God has a question for you right now, and it's the same question He asked Isaiah years ago: *"Then I heard the Lord asking, 'Whom should I send as a messenger to this people? Who will go for us?' I said, 'Here I am. Send me'"* (Isaiah 6:8).

You may be shaking your head in disagreement. Perhaps you haven't found a new job yet or that new business you're building hasn't yet come close to breaking even. You might think that disqualifies you from witnessing about God's blessings and His dominion over the workplace. If you're still waiting for your victory, hang in there. If you've found and planted your promises, you're talking to God every day, and you're at peace, then your victory is assured, wherever God leads you. You've got your seed in the ground and the harvest will come.

Without question, as you do the right things in your job search, walk in love and stay in a close relationship with God, you will be victorious. And, by the way, your present situation makes you perfectly qualified to testify about the Kingdom job search process. Recall that God is very protective of His reputation.

In the Old Testament, we read the conversation between God and Moses. Moses agreed with God that He had a right to kill all the Israelites because of their rebellious behavior, but Moses said that if God killed them, the rest of the world would question the value of following God.

According to Moses, these observers were likely to say: *"The Lord was not able to bring them into the land he swore to give them, so he killed them in the wilderness"* (Numbers 14:16).

For that reason alone, God decided to let that disobedient people live. How much more do you think God will preserve His reputation in partnership with believers who are willing and desiring to bring Him glory? So go ahead and declare the power of God over the workplace. Invite people to see what He will do in your life. You're not forcing God's hand when you do this; you're simply proclaiming His sovereignty over your life and your circumstances. *"It is written: 'I believed; therefore I have spoken.' With that same spirit of faith we also believe and therefore speak"* (2 Corinthians 4:13 NIV).

You could even go as far as I did and start serving Thanksgiving dinner in anticipation of your victory (just don't do it as often as I did if you want to continue to serve turkey to your family on future holidays)! The point is that you're someone others are watching right now. They want to see if your Kingdom job search is any different from what everyone else is experiencing. Share the peace and freedom from fear that you've discovered. Help others to break free, too.

But what if you haven't experienced the miraculous interventions I've talked about? Perhaps you're not at peace and you haven't experienced God's supernatural intervention in your situation yet. You may still be reading about God instead of encountering Him personally. It happens. There's a Kingdom solution for you as well.

Before we explore some options for you, be assured of this—the Word of God is powerful. It is not broken, and it applies to you. But God has His own timetable and most job seekers will agree that He is never early! Rest assured that He is never late either.

We believers are broken, and we experience failures even when we're giving it our very best shot. The good news is that we can be fixed and the Word of God doesn't need to be! So if you're still struggling, it could mean that your Kingdom job search dosage isn't right yet. Just as a doctor will adjust the strength of your medications until the right results are achieved, believers who aren't experiencing the success they are after should do the same. To transform your job search, there are three adjustments that you can try: involvement of others, performance appraisal, and stronghold identification and deliverance.

Let's start kicking up your dosage with the involvement of others. I remember a time in my life when everything was dry. I wasn't a new believer; I grew up with God and I thought my relationship with Him was as good as it could be. Still, I had no joy and no peace. When I prayed I heard nothing, and that frightened me. But in this time of great discomfort I cried out for help, and God brought me to anointed teachers of the Word. I was so very thirsty for the Truth and for a vital, personal relationship with Jesus. That's when God made the way for me to find what I was looking for. What He did for me He will surely do for you. So ask for teachers and resources to strengthen your faith and build your knowledge of God and the Laws of His Kingdom.

We are so very fortunate to live in this time. The Gospel has never been more accessible. You can find Kingdom instruction on television, radio and the Internet, 24 hours a day, seven days a week. The Bible is available on the Internet in multiple translations and in applications that make topic and word searches easy and readily available. If you're not computer savvy, chances are you know others who will help you and they'll be blessed by the experience as well. I bought an audio version of the Bible on CD and just started playing it every chance I got. Best of all, God has given us the Holy Spirit as our personal Guide and Teacher. So allow God to lead you in the study of His Word to find the answers you need. If you will seek and keep seeking, teachers will be provided and guidance will come.

Consider asking others to join you in this process as well. I can guarantee that you are not alone in your need for God's intervention in your employment situation, so start a job seekers or workplace support group. Many believers struggle as they try to make this journey on their own. You may be swimming upstream against false doctrines, a lack of knowledge of God's Word, or the criticism of those around you. You are not alone. And when you find others who are facing the same battles, you can join forces. Together you can explore God's promises, build your job search skills, and bring each other encouragement. *"A person standing alone can be attacked and defeated, but two can stand back-to-back and conquer. Three are even better, for a triple-braided cord is not easily broken"* (Ecclesiastes 4:12).

There's nothing very difficult about facilitating a two-hour meeting every week. Just open in prayer and give everyone two minutes to share what God has done in their lives over the past week. Keep your focus on God, by the way, and not the frustrations of the job search process! Review a discussion topic, read the related Scriptures, and invite everyone to talk about how the Word can

There's nothing very difficult about facilitating a two-hour meeting every week.

be applied to give direction to the job search situation. Finally, ask for prayer requests and hold each other accountable for praying in alignment with God's directions—*seeking Kingdom outcomes and God's expressed will.*

It's very helpful to the group when members share about the ways God has been faithful in answering prayer and touching their lives and circumstances. Then close your meeting in prayer and commit to keep praying for each other throughout the week. Why not take the first step and get a group of believers to join you as you explore God's plan for this time out of the workplace? God Himself promises to join your group, *"For where two or three gather together as my followers, I am there among them"* (Matthew 18:20).

In the hope that you are willing to share God's good news with other job seekers, there are Discussion Questions at the end of each chapter to guide and support your small group and get you started. I've also included a list of common job seeker questions and referenced the pages in this book that address each.

To help with the second adjustment option, a Performance Appraisal form can be found in the Appendix. It's good as a means for honestly assessing your activities in this season and can be a useful tool for small groups as well. As you and the other group members proceed through the job search process, it will help you to identify areas that need more attention. Use it as a reminder of the standards that we are measuring ourselves against as we seek to be excellent in a time of unemployment or misemployment, and make necessary changes in your job seeking process as needed.

But perhaps you have tried everything and you're just stuck. You recognize that you are not living in accordance with God's Word and you cannot find the strength to make the necessary changes. If you desire to turn your life and career over to God but still find yourself caught in unbelief, anxiety, depression, addiction, or sin, it's time to seek help. That's when the final adjustment, stronghold identification and deliverance, may be just what the doctor ordered.

Before continuing, allow me to clarify what we're talking about here. A stronghold is simply a lie that was accepted as the truth at some point in life. Over time, that deception became deeply entrenched and fortified. I'm sure you've heard of, or perhaps personally experienced, this type of lie. It's unfortunately too common that job seekers carry a belief established by trusted individuals, such as parents and teachers, who declared they would never amount to anything or were too stupid to get a good job. Many single women still suffer from tremendous guilt about going to work after their husbands have left them, believing that God is angry at them for working outside the home.

Once these strongholds are established, the believer never questions their validity. In fact most strongholds exist in believers' minds without their conscious awareness. Nevertheless, the presence of these strongholds can prevent job search progress and create perpetual problems in a believer's work-life. If you have been harboring any of these lies, you now have the opportunity to break free from their hold on your life.

Unfortunately, some lies have gotten into the church and have lead believers into strongholds of religious deception. Job seekers (and others!) have been told that it is up to them to figure out what they need, pick scriptures that solve the problem and claim them for themselves, and then speak them over and over in order to get the results they want. They've been told that this is "standing in faith." These are sincere Christians who think this is what God would have them do. Without knowing it, they have cut God entirely out of the process while trying to use the Word as some kind of recipe book.

When these job seekers fail to get the expected results, they become disillusioned and crushed, thinking that somehow they're failing to perform up to God's standard. They question the strength of their faith, the sincerity of their belief in Jesus, and God's love for them. By correcting this erroneous teaching and helping them to get into a personal relationship with God, in prayer, they experience such relief. For the first time, they are able to shift the entire load they've been carrying onto God's shoulders and allow Him to show them the solutions they need. It is amazing how comforting it can be to realize that it's not up to us to figure everything out, that we have a Father who has already done that and all we have to do is seek Him for our answers and get into His will to find peace and purpose.

There's a second group of believers who have also been trained to cut God out without knowing it. These are believers who don't personally seek God for anything. They hurl prayers at Him but never listen or expect answers. They beg for the things they want but end every prayer with the words "if it's Your will" and then just go on about their business. Again, this looks like Christian behavior, but it is completely missing the process of getting to know God personally. They have never learned to actually recognize His voice and discover His will for their lives. Some are actually persuaded that it isn't even possible to know God personally, so they have settled for just reading about Him.

It is so wonderful to see what happens as these job seekers start to study God's Word, expecting to find answers to their needs and begin to listen for His voice in prayer. There's such excitement when they receive personal direction and experience the love of Christ, sometimes for the very first time in their entire Christian walk. God becomes real and they learn to trust that He will always care enough to answer when they cry out to Him.

As I work in this ministry, I meet job seekers who suffer from strongholds of worldly origin as well. Some have been so inundated with the lies of this world that they have unknowingly accepted beliefs that do not line up with the Word of God. Some of the more common lies job seekers accept are:

- "No one will hire you if you've been out of work for more than a year."
- "You won't find work if you're over 40."
- "There are no jobs in this area."
- "You'll never overcome it if you have a felony on your record."

While this might be true in the world's economy, it isn't true for the children of God. The Bible is full of stories that reveal how God's economy has prevailed in times of famine, economic crisis and hardship.

Others have needed guidance in order to recognize a stronghold of sin in their lives. With help they discovered that they had been holding onto pride, envy, greed, addiction or some other sin that was holding them captive and preventing their progress.

Look at what Jesus said about unforgiveness. *"For if you forgive men their trespasses, your heavenly Father will also forgive you. But if you do not forgive men their trespasses, neither will your Father forgive your trespasses"* (Matthew 6:14-15 NKJV). The apostle Paul tells us, *"And do not bring sorrow to God's Holy Spirit by the way you live. Remember, he has identified you as his own, guaranteeing that you will be saved on the day of redemption. Get rid of all bitterness, rage, anger, harsh words, and slander, as well as all types of evil behavior. Instead, be kind to each other, tenderhearted, forgiving one another, just as God through Christ has forgiven you"* (Ephesians 4:30-32). So, clearly it's important that we work to remove sinful behaviors from our lives.

"Instead, be kind to each other, tenderhearted, forgiving one another, just as God through Christ has forgiven you."

Even the medical profession now recognizes that harboring emotions such as bitterness and unforgiveness can also lead to stress, depression, and even physical diseases that can compound the job seekers' challenges. Unknowingly, many have permitted themselves to nurture unforgiveness towards a past employer until it seems like the reasonable and natural way to think and behave and yet, it is a stronghold that can keep them from the blessing God has in mind for them. Paul warns, *"Don't you know that when you offer yourselves to someone to obey him as slaves, you are slaves to the one whom you obey—whether you are slaves to sin, which leads to death, or to obedience, which leads to righteousness?"* (Romans 6:16 NIV). Once they recognized and repented of the sin that was holding them captive, they were able to move forward.

As we leave this topic, I am reminded of 2 Corinthians 10:3-5: *"For though we walk in the flesh, we do not war according to the flesh. For the weapons of our warfare are not carnal but mighty in God for pulling down strongholds, casting down arguments and every high thing that exalts itself against the knowledge of God, bringing every thought into captivity to the obedience of Christ"* (NKJV).

So if you're stuck, understand that it's not only critical to study God's Word but also to practice the discipline of continuously correcting your thoughts in order to uproot lies that can become strongholds. I don't personally know anything more powerful than seeking God, in prayer, and asking Him to show the way out. To guide you through this process, God may lead you to a Christian counselor or a mature believer who's experienced in helping afflicted believers. So, be open to that possibility. The point is, don't stay stuck; reach out for help.

With that work behind you, go back to your job search and continue with the Kingdom plan. Get into God's Word, seek His guidance and get on with the business of building your skills as a job seeker. God will do the rest.

CHAPTER EIGHT

1. What does God expect of us at the completion of a Kingdom job search?

2. What can we do, if anything, to speed up a job search process and move into our next assignment?

3. What can we do if we're not getting the results we need from our job search? (Discuss all three adjustments.)

4. How should our Kingdom citizenship affect our behavior after we get new jobs and businesses?

CONCLUSION

> *"Then the Lord answered me and said: 'Write the vision and make it plain on tablets, that he may run who reads it'"* (Habakkuk 2:2 NKJV).

This is what I have attempted to do with *Employed for Life: "When Can You Start?" -God.* It is my prayer that you have discovered the powerful, practical application of the Word of God in your personal employment situation. This remains God's promise to all who will receive it. If you haven't yet, don't worry. It's a process, not an event. Just continue to work the exercises in this book. It will come. God always keeps His promises.

> *"No longer will they build houses and others live in them, or plant and others eat. For as the days of a tree, so will be the days of my people; my chosen ones will long enjoy the works of their hands"* (Isaiah 65:22 NIV).

Beyond your employment situation and work, I hope your life will also be transformed so that you may walk in the Kingdom of God. May your life journey be blessed and may you freely share the truth you now possess with the world of people who still need to hear the Good News.

APPENDIX

JOB SEARCH PERFORMANCE APPRAISAL

If you are willing to be completely honest with yourself, this evaluation can help you to identify those areas that need your attention in order to get the success you want. Give yourself four points for every statement that accurately reflects your current job search behavior.

Priority

__ I spend time with God, in His Word, every day.

__ I pray with Kingdom motives of love and purpose as God leads me.

__ I give thanks at all times.

__ I praise God continually for all that He is and has done in my life.

__ I have identified the Word promises that answer my prayer needs and I speak them out loud often.

__ I guard my speech and my thoughts to keep them in line with God's Word.

Discipline

__ I have a balanced daily routine and I stick to it.

__ I give away my time and talents on a consistent basis.

__ I am completing projects that I could not have accomplished while working.

__ I treat my body as a temple of the Holy Spirit and God's property.

__ I am walking in love and without strife in every part of my life.

Job Search

__ I have prepared and practiced my answers to the following questions: "Why are you unemployed?" "Tell me about yourself?" "What type of work are you looking for?" and "What salary do you want?"

__ I have a written CAR (Conditions/Actions/Results) story to prove every one of my transferable and work skills as well as my key accomplishments.

__ I have compiled a list of everyone I know and contacted them for employment leads.

__ Every call I make creates a favorable impression and produces two more names to call; my network is continuously growing.

__ I spend the majority of my time searching in the "hidden job market," making contacts before positions are advertised.

Battle

__ I have sought and destroyed enemy strongholds in my mind.

__ My mind has been, and continues to be, renewed by the study of God's Word.

__ I have banished every form of fear from my life.

__ I put on the full armor of God every day before I begin my activities.

__ I protect my life, job search activities, and loved ones with God's protective promises.

__ My family is well covered by my prayers.

Kingdom

__ I conduct myself as an ambassador for Jesus Christ and representative of God's Kingdom.

__ I pray for every person and business that I encounter.

__ I look for ways to be of service and treat others with the love of Christ wherever I go.

__ I obey God whenever He directs me to share my testimony or demonstrate His Kingdom.

__ I continue to give and to bless and, thereby, open myself to God's blessing (Luke 6:38).

Evaluate your performance:

Each item on this appraisal is worth 4 points. A passing score for a Kingdom job seeker is 100%.

In other words, every one of these elements is within your control and essential to a successful Kingdom job search. These behaviors and activities are designed to give you a victory in your job search and transform your life permanently. If you've been letting yourself slide in any of these areas, repent and commit yourself anew to the process. God has the five-fold blessing for you. It's just up to you to claim it!

25 FREQUENTLY ASKED QUESTIONS

1. Why did God do this to me? Why did God let this happen?
   Chapter 2, pp. 27-29

2. What does it mean to "Seek first the Kingdom"?
   Chapter 4

3. What if I deserved to be fired? What if I really did something wrong?
   Chapter 2, p. 28; Chapter 3, p. 69

4. Should I sue my former employer or try to get my old job back?
   Chapter 3, p. 68

5. How am I going to make it financially? How will I be able to financially support my unemployed spouse (family, self)?
   Chapter 1, p. 18; Chapter 4, p. 54; Chapter 7, pp. 175, 187

6. What does God require of me during this process of unemployment?
   Chapter 7, pp. 174-175

7. Where do I start?
   Chapter 3

8. What is my purpose? What does God want me to do?
   Chapter 6

9. How can I discover my design, my gifts, my talents...? What are my marketable skills?
   Chapter 5, pp. 122-124

10. What if I can't find a good job? What if I'm too old or fat or illiterate or...?
    Chapter 5, pp. 61-62

11. What if I don't have a job objective? What if I don't really know what I want?
    Chapter 5

12. How do I know if I'm hearing from God? (Is it me, is it God, or is it the Enemy?)
    Chapter 7, pp. 176-178

13. How do I know if I'm doing the right things?
    Chapter 7

14. Why isn't God speaking to me? Why can't I hear God?
    Chapter 7, p. 178

15. How can I get the support of my spouse (family, friends…)?
    Chapter 7, pp. 183-185

16. How can I stop the devil from interfering with my job search?
    Chapter 3; Chapter 6; Chapter 7, pp, 183-184

17. How long is this going to take? How can I speed it up?
    Chapter 7, pp. 175-176

18. Should I just take "any job" or should I keep looking for the "great job"?
    Chapter 5, pp. 118-120

19. What salary will I make? Do I have to go backwards?
    Chapter 7, pp. 198-199

20. What if the job I want won't pay the amount I need to support myself and my family?
    Chapter 2, p. 38; Chapter 5, pp. 113-115

21. How can I measure my progress? Am I gaining on it?
    Chapter 7, pp. 178-180

22. What's wrong with me? Why is this taking so long?
    Chapter 7

23. How can I overcome the depression that's keeping me from finding a job?
    Chapter 8

24. How do I deal with a sense of worthlessness?
    Chapter 4

25. How can I present a better witness or be a more excellent demonstration than a job seeker who doesn't know Jesus?
    Chapter 4, p. 86; Chapter 7; Chapter 8, pp. 204-206

LIST OF SCRIPTURAL REFERENCES

Chapter One:

John 10:9 (NKJV) I am the door. If anyone enters by me, he will be saved, and will go in and out and find pasture.

Matthew 5:45 (NLT) For he gives his sunlight to both the evil and the good, and he sends rain on the just and the unjust alike.

Philippians 1:6 (NLT) ...that God, who began the good work within you, will continue his work until it is finally finished on the day when Christ Jesus returns.

Ephesians 1:19-23 (NLT) I also pray that you will understand the incredible greatness of God's power for us who believe him. This is the same mighty power that raised Christ from the dead and seated him in the place of honor at God's right hand in the heavenly realms. Now he is far above any ruler or authority or power or leader or anything else—not only in this world but also in the world to come. God has put all things under the authority of Christ and has made him head over all things for the benefit of the church. And the church is his body; it is made full and complete by Christ, who fills all things everywhere with himself.

Philippians 2:9-10 (NKJV) Therefore God also has highly exalted him and given Him the name which is above every name, that at the name of Jesus every knee should bow, of those in heaven, and of those on earth, and of those under the earth.

Genesis 50:20 (NKJV) ...you meant evil against me; but God meant it for good....

Psalm 139:14 (NKJV) ...I am fearfully and wonderfully made....

Romans 12:3 (NKJV) For I say, through the grace given to me, to everyone who is among you, not to think of himself more highly than he ought to think....

1 John 4:17 (NKJV) Love has been perfected among us in this: that we may have boldness in the day of judgment; because as He is, so are we in this world.

Ecclesiastes 3:12-13 (NIV) I know that there is nothing better for men than to be happy and do good while they live. That everyone may eat and drink, and find satisfaction in all his toil — this is the gift of God.

Ephesians 3:20 (NLT) Now all glory to God, who is able, through his mighty power at work within us, to accomplish infinitely more than we might ask or think.

Luke 11:9-10 (NLT) "And so I tell you, keep on asking, and you will receive what you ask for. Keep on seeking, and you will find. Keep on knocking, and the door will be opened to you. For everyone who asks, receives. Everyone who seeks, finds. And to everyone who knocks, the door will be opened.

Proverbs 15:23 (NLT) Everyone enjoys a fitting reply; it is wonderful to say the right thing at the right time!

Isaiah 54:17 (NLT) But in that coming day no weapon turned against you will succeed. You will silence every voice raised up to accuse you. These benefits are enjoyed by the servants of the Lord; their vindication will come from me. I, the Lord, have spoken!

Chapter Two:

Jeremiah 29:11 (NLT) "For I know the plans I have for you," says the Lord. "They are plans for good and not for disaster, to give you a future and a hope.

John 10:10 (NKJV) I have come that they may have life and that they may have it more abundantly.

1 Peter 5:8 (NKJV) Be sober, be vigilant; because your adversary the devil walks about like a roaring lion, seeking whom he may devour.

Matthew 7:9 (NKJV) Or what man is there among you who, if his son asks for bread, will give him a stone?

Hebrews 8:6 (NKJV) But now He has obtained a more excellent ministry, inasmuch as He is also Mediator of a better covenant, which was established on better promises.

Romans 8:2 (NKJV) For the law of the Spirit of life in Christ Jesus has made me free from the law of sin and death.

Romans 8:28 (NKJV) And we know that all things work together for good to those who love God, to those who are the called according to His purpose.

Isaiah 41:10 (NKJV) Fear not, for I am with you; Be not dismayed, for I am your God. I will strengthen you, Yes, I will help you, I will uphold you with my righteous right hand.

1 John 3:8 (NKJV) He who sins is of the devil, for the devil has sinned from the beginning. For this purpose the Son of God was manifested, that He might destroy the works of the devil.

Genesis 18:14 (NKJV) Is anything too hard for the Lord? At the appointed time I will return to you, according to the time of life, and Sarah shall have a son."

Matthew 11:28 (NLT) Then Jesus said, "Come to me, all of you who are weary and carry heavy burdens, and I will give you rest.

Romans 9:17 (NLT) For the Scriptures say that God told Pharaoh, "I have appointed you for the very purpose of displaying my power in you and to spread my fame throughout the earth."

Luke 10:42 (NLT) There is only one thing worth being concerned about. Mary has discovered it and it will not be taken away from her.

Psalm 121:7 (NIV) The Lord will keep you from all harm-He will watch over your life.

Psalm 103:3-5 (NKJV) Who forgives all your iniquities, Who heals all your diseases, Who redeems your life from destruction, Who crowns you with lovingkindness and tender mercies, Who satisfies your mouth with good things, So that your youth is renewed like the eagle's.

Matthew 6:33 (NLT) Seek the Kingdom of God above all else, and live righteously, and he will give you everything you need.

Chapter Three:

Isaiah 41:10 (NKJV) Fear not, for I am with you; Be not dismayed, for I am your God. I will strengthen you, Yes, I will help you, I will uphold you with My righteous right hand.

2 Timothy 1:7 (NKJV) For God has not given us a spirit of fear, but of power and of love and of a sound mind.

2 Corinthians 10:4 (NIV) The weapons we fight with are not the weapons of the world. On the contrary, they have divine power to demolish strongholds.

Matthew 11:12 (NKJV) And from the days of John the Baptist until now the kingdom of heaven suffers violence, and the violent take it by force.

1 John 4:18 (NLT) Such love has no fear, because perfect love expels all fear. If we are afraid, it is for fear of punishment, and this shows that we have not fully experienced his perfect love.

2 Timothy 1:7 (NLT) For God has not given us a spirit of fear and timidity, but of power, love, and self-discipline.

Luke 12:22-26 (NLT) Then, turning to his disciples, Jesus said, "That is why I tell you not to worry about everyday life—whether you have enough food to eat or enough clothes to wear. For life is more than food, and your body more than clothing. Look at the ravens. They don't plant or harvest or store food in barns, for God feeds them. And you are far more valuable to him than any birds! Can all your worries add a single moment to your life? And if worry can't accomplish a little thing like that, what's the use of worrying over bigger things?

1 Peter 5:7 (NLT) Give all your worries and cares to God, for he cares about you.

Luke 1:74 (NLT) We have been rescued from our enemies so we can serve God without fear,

Isaiah 43:1 (NKJV) But now, thus says the Lord, who created you, O Jacob, And He who formed you, O Israel: "Fear not, for I have redeemed you; I have called you by your name; You are Mine.

Psalm 127:2 (NLT) It is useless for you to work so hard from early morning until late at night, anxiously working for food to eat; for God gives rest to his loved ones.

Psalm 91:5 (NLT) Do not be afraid of the terrors of the night, nor the arrow that flies in the day.

Isaiah 54:14 (NLT) You will be secure under a government that is just and fair. Your enemies will stay far away. You will live in peace, and terror will not come near.

Jeremiah 51:46 (NLT) But do not panic; don't be afraid when you hear the first rumor of approaching forces. For rumors will keep coming year by year. Violence will erupt in the land as the leaders fight against each other.

Deuteronomy 20:3 (NIV) He shall say: "Hear, O Israel, today you are going into battle against your enemies. Do not be fainthearted or afraid; do not be terrified or give way to panic before them.

Job 3:25 (NIV) What I feared has come upon me; what I dreaded has happened to me.

Luke 8:49 (NKJV) Someone came from the ruler of the synagogue's house, saying to him, "Your daughter is dead. Do not trouble the Teacher." But when Jesus heard it, He answered him, saying, "Do not be afraid; only believe, and she will be made well."

Philippians 4:19 (NLT) And this same God who takes care of me will supply all your needs from his glorious riches, which have been given to us in Christ Jesus.

Hebrews 10:35 (NIV) So do not throw away your confidence; it will be richly rewarded.

Ecclesiastes 4:12 (NLT) A person standing alone can be attacked and defeated, but two can stand back-to-back and conquer. Three are even better, for a triple-braided cord is not easily broken.

Deuteronomy 32:35 (NLT) I will take revenge; I will pay them back. In due time their feet will slip. Their day of disaster will arrive, and their destiny will overtake them.

Isaiah 43:18-19 (NIV) Forget the former things; do not dwell on the past. See, I am doing a new thing! Now it springs up; do you not perceive it? I am making a way in the desert and streams in the wasteland.

Ephesians 4:17-18 (NLT) With the Lord's authority I say this: Live no longer as the Gentiles do, for they are hopelessly confused. Their minds are full of darkness; they wander far from the life God gives because they have closed their minds and hardened their hearts against him.

Ephesians 6:11-17 (NIV) Put on the full armor of God so that you can take your stand against the devil's schemes. For our struggle is not against flesh and blood, but against the rulers, against the authorities, against the powers of this dark world and against the spiritual forces of evil in the heavenly realms. Therefore put on the full armor of God, so that when the day of evil comes, you may be able to stand your ground, and after you have done everything, to stand. Stand firm then, with the belt of truth buckled around your waist, with the breastplate of righteousness in place, and with your feet fitted with the readiness that comes from the gospel of peace. In addition to all this, take up the shield of faith, with which you can extinguish all the flaming arrows of the evil one. Take the helmet of salvation and the sword of the Spirit, which is the word of God.

2 Chronicles 20:22-24 (NLT) At the very moment they began to sing and give praise, the Lord caused the armies of Ammon, Moab, and Mount Seir to start fighting among themselves. The armies of Moab and Ammon turned against their allies from Mount Seir and killed every one of them. After they had destroyed the army of Seir, they began attacking each other. So when the army of Judah arrived at the lookout point in the wilderness, all they saw were dead bodies lying on the ground as far as they could see. Not a single one of the enemy had escaped.

Acts 12:5-10 (NLT) But while Peter was in prison, the church prayed very earnestly for him. The night before Peter was to be placed on trial, he was asleep, fastened with two chains between two soldiers. Others stood guard at the prison gate. Suddenly, there was a bright light in the cell, and an angel of the Lord stood before Peter. The angel struck him on the side to awaken him and said, "Quick! Get up!" And the chains fell off his wrists. Then the angel told him, "Get dressed and put on your sandals." And he did. "Now put on your coat and follow me," the angel ordered. So Peter left the cell, following the angel. But all the time he thought it was a vision. He didn't realize it was actually happening. They passed the first and second guard posts and came to the iron gate leading to the city, and this opened for them all by itself. So they passed through and started walking down the street, and then the angel suddenly left him.

2 Kings 6:16-17 (NIV) "Don't be afraid," the prophet answered. "Those who are with us are more than those who are with them." And Elisha prayed, "O Lord, open his eyes so he may see." Then the Lord opened the servant's eyes, and he looked and saw the hills full of horses and chariots of fire all around Elisha.

Psalm 91:11 (NKJV) For He shall give His angels charge over you, to keep you in all your ways.

Philippians 3:13-14 (NLT) No, dear brothers and sisters, I have not achieved it, but I focus on this one thing: Forgetting the past and looking forward to what lies ahead, I press on to reach the end of the race and receive the heavenly prize for which God, through Christ Jesus, is calling us.

James 1:2-4 (NIV) Consider it pure joy, my brothers, whenever you face trials of many kinds, because you know that the testing of your faith develops perseverance. Perseverance must finish its work so that you may be mature and complete, not lacking anything.

Philippians 3:13-14 (NIV) Brothers, I do not consider myself yet to have taken hold of it. But one thing I do: Forgetting what is behind and straining toward what is ahead, I press on toward the goal to win the prize for which God has called me heavenward in Christ Jesus.

Chapter Four:

Matthew 6:31-33 (NIV) So do not worry, saying, 'What shall we eat?' or 'What shall we drink?' or 'What shall we wear?' For the pagans run after all these things, and your heavenly Father knows that you need them. But seek first his kingdom and his righteousness, and all these things will be given to you as well.

Luke 22:35 (NKJV) And He said to them, "When I sent you without money bag, knapsack, and sandals, did you lack anything? So they said, "Nothing."

Colossians 1:11-14 (NLT) ...May you be filled with joy, always thanking the Father. He has enabled you to share in the inheritance that belongs to his people, who live in the light. For he has rescued us from the kingdom of darkness and transferred us into the Kingdom of his dear Son, who purchased our freedom and forgave our sins.

Ephesians 1:4 (NLT) Even before He made the world, God loved us and chose us in Christ to be holy and without fault in his eyes.

John 15:16 (NLT) You didn't choose me. I chose you. I appointed you to go and produce lasting fruit, so that the Father will give you whatever you ask for, using my name.

Hebrews 2:8-10 (NLT) You gave them authority over all things. Now when it says "all things," it means nothing is left out. But we have not yet seen all things put under their authority. What we do see is Jesus, who was given a position "a little lower than the angels"; and because he suffered death for us, he is now "crowned with glory and honor." Yes, by God's grace, Jesus tasted death for everyone. God, for whom and through whom everything was made, chose to bring many children into glory. And it was only right that he should make Jesus, through his suffering, a perfect leader, fit to bring them into their salvation.

Ephesians 1:19-23 (NLT) I also pray that you will understand the incredible greatness of God's power for us who believe him. This is the same mighty power that raised Christ from the dead and seated him in the place of honor at God's right hand in the heavenly realms. Now he is far above any ruler or authority or power or leader or anything else — not only in this world but also in the world to come. God has put all things under the authority of Christ and has made him head over all things for the benefit of the church. And the church is his body; it is made full and complete by Christ, who fills all things everywhere with himself.

1 John 3:2 (NLT) Dear friends, we are already God's children, but he has not yet shown us what we will be like when Christ appears. But we do know that we will be like him, for we will see him as he really is.

1 Corinthians 6:19-20 (NKJV) Or do you not know that your body is a temple of the Holy Spirit who is in you, whom you have from God, and you are not your own? You were bought at a price; therefore glorify God in your body and in your spirit, which are God's.

Matthew 6:24 (NLT) No one can serve two masters. For you will hate one and love the other; you will be devoted to one and despise the other....

Joshua 24:15 (NIV) But if serving the Lord seems undesirable to you, then choose for yourselves this day whom you will serve, whether the gods your forefathers served beyond the River, or the gods of the Amorites, in whose land you are living. But as for me and my household, we will serve the Lord.

Hebrews 2:10 (NLT) God, for whom and through whom everything was made, chose to bring many children into glory. And it was only right that he should make Jesus, through his suffering, a perfect leader, fit to bring them into their salvation.

Ephesians 1:4 (NLT) Even before he made the world, God loved us and chose us in Christ to be holy and without fault in his eyes.

Luke 12:32 (NLT) So don't be afraid, little flock. For it gives your Father great happiness to give you the Kingdom.

James 4:8 (NKJV) Draw near to God and He will draw near to you. Cleanse your hands, you sinners; and purify your hearts, you double-minded.

Luke 11:10 (NLT) For everyone who asks, receives. Everyone who seeks, finds. And to everyone who knocks, the door will be opened.

Acts 17:26-28 (NIV) From one man he made every nation of men, that they should inhabit the whole earth; and He determined the times set for them and the exact places where they should live. God did this so that men would seek him and perhaps reach out for him, and find him, though he is not far from each one of us. 'For in him we live and move and have our being.' As some of your own poets have said, 'We are His offspring.'

Hebrews 11.6 (NKJV) But without faith it is impossible to please Him, for he who comes to God must believe that He is, and that He is a rewarder of those who diligently seek Him.

Proverbs 18:21 (NLT) The tongue can bring death or life; those who love to talk will reap the consequences.

Mark 10:27 (NLT) Jesus looked at them intently and said, "Humanly speaking, it is impossible. But not with God. Everything is possible with God."

Luke 14:28-33 (NLT) "But don't begin until you count the cost. For who would begin construction of a building without first calculating the cost to see if there is enough money to finish it? Otherwise, you might complete only the foundation before running out of money, and then everyone would laugh at you. They would say, 'There's the person who started that building and couldn't afford to finish it!' Or what king would go to war against another king without first sitting down with his counselors to discuss whether his army of 10,000 could defeat the 20,000 soldiers marching against him? And if he can't, he will send a delegation to discuss terms of peace while the enemy is still far away. So you cannot become my disciple without giving up everything you own."

Matthew 6:24 (NLT) No one can serve two masters. For you will hate one and love the other; you will be devoted to one and despise the other. You cannot serve both God and money.

Matthew 7:9-11 (NIV) Which of you, if his son asks for bread, will give him a stone? Or if he asks for a fish, will give him a snake? If you, then, though you are evil, know how to give good gifts to your children, how much more will your Father in heaven give good gifts to those who ask him!

Matthew 6:31-33 (NLT) "So don't worry about these things, saying, 'What will we eat? What will we drink? What will we wear?' These things dominate the thoughts of unbelievers, but your heavenly Father already knows all your needs. Seek the Kingdom of God above all else, and live righteously, and he will give you everything you need."

Romans 8:19 (NIV) The creation waits in eager expectation for the sons of God to be revealed.

Romans 12:2 (NLT) Don't copy the behavior and customs of this world, but let God transform you into a new person by changing the way you think. Then you will learn to know God's will for you, which is good and pleasing and perfect.

Philippians 4:19 (NLT) And this same God who takes care of me will supply all your needs from his glorious riches, which have been given to us in Christ Jesus.

John 10:7-15 (NLT) So he explained it to them: "I tell you the truth, I am the gate for the sheep... Those who come in through me will be saved. They will come and go freely and will find good pastures. The thief's purpose is to steal and kill and destroy. My purpose is to give them a rich and satisfying life. I am the good shepherd. The good shepherd sacrifices his life for the sheep. A hired hand will run when he sees a wolf coming. He will abandon the sheep because they don't belong to him and he isn't their shepherd. And so the wolf attacks them and scatters the flock. The hired hand runs away because he's working only for the money and doesn't really care about the sheep. I am the good shepherd; I know my own sheep, and they know me, just as my Father knows me and I know the Father. So I sacrifice my life for the sheep."

John 14:21 (NLT) Those who accept my commandments and obey them are the ones who love me. And because they love me, my Father will love them. And I will love them and reveal myself to each of them."

John 8:31 (NKJV) Then Jesus said to those Jews who believed Him, "If you abide in My word, you are My disciples indeed.

Hebrews 11:6 (NLT) And it is impossible to please God without faith. Anyone who wants to come to him must believe that God exists and that he rewards those who sincerely seek him.

1 Timothy 5:18 (NIV) For the Scripture says, "Do not muzzle the ox while it is treading out the grain," and "The worker deserves his wages."

Psalm 34:10 (NLT) Even strong young lions sometimes go hungry, but those who trust in the Lord will lack no good thing.

2 Corinthians 9:8 (NIV) And God is able to make all grace abound to you, so that in all things at all times, having all that you need, you will abound in every good work.

Isaiah 46:4 (NLT) I will be your God throughout your lifetime—until your hair is white with age. I made you, and I will care for you. I will carry you along and save you.

Matthew 11:28 (NLT) Then Jesus said, "Come to me, all of you who are weary and carry heavy burdens, and I will give you rest.

Luke 6:38 (NIV) Give, and it will be given to you. A good measure, pressed down, shaken together and running over, will be poured into your lap. For with the measure you use, it will be measured to you.

Jeremiah 33:6 (NIV) 'Nevertheless, I will bring health and healing to it; I will heal my people and will let them enjoy abundant peace and security.

Matthew 7:2 (NLT) For you will be treated as you treat others.

Psalm 19:14 (NKJV) Let the words of my mouth and the meditation of my heart, Be acceptable in Your sight, O Lord, my strength and my Redeemer.

James 2:8 (NLT) Yes indeed, it is good when you obey the royal law as found in the Scriptures: "Love your neighbor as yourself."

Matthew 5:37 (NIV) Simply let your 'Yes' be 'Yes,' and your 'No,' 'No'; anything beyond this comes from the evil one.

Ephesians 6:7 (NIV) Serve wholeheartedly, as if you were serving the Lord, not men,

Proverbs 10:9 (NLT) People with integrity walk safely, but those who follow crooked paths will slip and fall.

Chapter Five:

Proverbs 2:3-5 (NLT) Cry out for insight, and ask for understanding. Search for them as you would for silver; seek them like hidden treasures. Then you will understand what it means to fear the Lord, and you will gain knowledge of God.

Matthew 21:22 (NKJV) And whatever things you ask in prayer, believing, you will receive.

John 14:13 (NLT) You can ask for anything in my name, and I will do it, so that the Son can bring glory to the Father.

John 15:16 (NLT) You didn't choose me. I chose you. I appointed you to go and produce lasting fruit, so that the Father will give you whatever you ask for, using my name.

1 John 5:15 (NLT) And since we know he hears us when we make our requests, we also know that he will give us what we ask for.

Matthew 6:8 (NKJV) Therefore do not be like them. For your Father knows the things you have need of before you ask Him.

Matthew 6:31-33 (NIV) So do not worry, saying, 'What shall we eat?' or 'What shall we drink?' or 'What shall we wear?' For the pagans run after all these things, and your heavenly Father knows that you need them. But seek first his kingdom and his righteousness, and all these things will be given to you as well.

Proverbs 2:3-5 (NLT) Cry out for insight, and ask for understanding. Search for them as you would for silver; seek them like hidden treasures. Then you will understand what it means to fear the Lord, and you will gain knowledge of God.

James 5:16 (NKJV) Confess your trespasses to one another, and pray for one another, that you may be healed. The effective, fervent prayer of a righteous man avails much.

John 12:49 (NLT) I don't speak on my own authority. The Father who sent me has commanded me what to say and how to say it.

James 4.3 (NLT) And even when you ask, you don't get it because your motives are all wrong—you want only what will give you pleasure.

Romans 12:3 (NKJV) For I say, through the grace given to me, to everyone who is among you, not to think of himself more highly than he ought to think, but to think soberly, as God has dealt to each one a measure of faith.

Luke 12:12 (NKJV) For the Holy Spirit will teach you in that very hour what you ought to say.

Galatians 3:29 (NKJV) And if you are Christ's, then you are Abraham's seed, and heirs according to the promise.

2 Timothy 2:15 (NLT) Work hard so you can present yourself to God and receive his approval. Be a good worker, one who does not need to be ashamed and who correctly explains the word of truth.

Psalm 37:4 (NLT) Take delight in the Lord, and he will give you your heart's desires.

Matthew 21:22 (NLT) You can pray for anything, and if you have faith, you will receive it.

Mark 5:36 (NKJV) As soon as Jesus heard the word that was spoken, He said to the ruler of the synagogue, "Do not be afraid; only believe."

1 John 5:15 (NLT) And since we know he hears us when we make our requests, we also know that he will give us what we ask for.

Matthew 21:22 (NKJV) And whatever things you ask in prayer, believing, you will receive.

John 14:13 (NLT) You can ask for anything in my name, and I will do it, so that the Son can bring glory to the Father.

John 15:16 (NLT) You didn't choose me. I chose you. I appointed you to go and produce lasting fruit, so that the Father will give you whatever you ask for, using my name.

Luke 11:9-10 (NLT) And so I tell you, keep on asking, and you will receive what you ask for. Keep on seeking, and you will find. Keep on knocking, and the door will be opened to you. For everyone who asks, receives. Everyone who seeks, finds. And to everyone who knocks, the door will be opened.

Isaiah 40.31 (NLT) But those who trust in the Lord will find new strength. They will soar high on wings like eagles. They will run and not grow weary. They will walk and not faint.

James 5:16 (NLT) The earnest prayer of a righteous person has great power and produces wonderful results.

2 Timothy 2:15 (NKJV) Be diligent to present yourself approved to God, a worker who does not need to be ashamed, rightly dividing the word of truth.

Chapter Six:

Proverbs 3:5-6 (NLT) Trust in the Lord with all your heart; do not depend on your own understanding. Seek his will in all you do, and he will show you which path to take."

Isaiah 40:28-31 (NLT) Have you never heard? Have you never understood? The Lord is the everlasting God, the Creator of all the earth. He never grows weak or weary. No one can measure the depths of his understanding. He gives power to the weak and strength to the powerless. Even youths will become weak and tired, and young men will fall in exhaustion. But those who trust in the Lord will find new strength. They will soar high on wings like eagles. They will run and not grow weary. They will walk and not faint.

Isaiah 41:10 (NKJV) Fear not, for I am with you. Be not dismayed, for I am your God. I will strengthen you, Yes, I will help you, I will uphold you with my righteous right hand.'

Matthew 14.31 (NIV) Immediately Jesus reached out his hand and caught him. "You of little faith," He said, "why did you doubt?"

Ephesians 3:16-19 (NLT) I pray that from his glorious, unlimited resources he will empower you with inner strength through his Spirit. Then Christ will make his home in your hearts as you trust in him. Your roots will grow down into God's love and keep you strong. And may you have the power to understand, as all God's people should, how wide, how long, how high, and how deep his love is. May you experience the love of Christ, though it is too great to understand fully. Then you will be made complete with all the fullness of life and power that comes from God.

Nehemiah 4:17-18 (NIV) ...Those who carried materials did their work with one hand and held a weapon in the other, and each of the builders wore his sword at his side as he worked. But the man who sounded the trumpet stayed with me.

1 Peter 5:8 (NLT) Stay alert! Watch out for your great enemy, the devil. He prowls around like a roaring lion, looking for someone to devour.

Luke 11:9-10 (NLT) "And so I tell you, keep on asking, and you will receive what you ask for. Keep on seeking, and you will find. Keep on knocking, and the door will be opened to you. For everyone who asks, receives. Everyone who seeks, finds. And to everyone who knocks, the door will be opened.

2 Timothy 2:15 (NIV) Do your best to present yourself to God as one approved, a workman who does not need to be ashamed and who correctly handles the word of truth.

James 2:14 (NLT) What good is it, dear brothers and sisters, if you say you have faith but don't show it by your actions? Can that kind of faith save anyone?

Romans 12:10-12 (NKJV) Be kindly affectionate to one another with brotherly love, in honor giving preference to one another; not lagging in diligence, fervent in spirit, serving the Lord; rejoicing in hope, patient in tribulation, continuing steadfastly in prayer.

John 8:32,36 (NKJV) And you shall know the truth, and the truth shall make you free…. Therefore if the Son makes you free, you shall be free indeed.

Psalm 91:1,4,9-10 (NKJV) He who dwells in the secret place of the Most High shall abide under the shadow of the Almighty.... He shall cover you with His feathers, And under His wings you shall take refuge; Because you have made the Lord, who is my refuge, Even the Most High, your dwelling place, No evil shall befall you, Nor shall any plague come near your dwelling;

John 13:35 (NKJV) By this all will know that you are my disciples, if you have love for one another.

Psalm 37:25 (NIV) I was young and now I am old, yet I have never seen the righteous forsaken or their children begging bread. They are always generous and lend freely; their children will be blessed.

2 Corinthians 5:7 (NKJV) For we walk by faith, not by sight.

Isaiah 30:21 (NKJV) Your ears shall hear a word behind you, saying, "This is the way, walk in it," Whenever you turn to the right hand Or whenever you turn to the left.

1 Samuel 30:6 (NKJV) Now David was greatly distressed, for the people spoke of stoning him, because the soul of all the people was grieved, every man for his sons and his daughters. But David strengthened himself in the Lord his God.

Nehemiah 8:10 (NKJV) Then he said to them, "Go your way, eat the fat, drink the sweet, and send portions to those for whom nothing is prepared; for this day is holy to our Lord. Do not sorrow, for the joy of the Lord is your strength."

Psalm 28:7 (NIV) The Lord is my strength and my shield; my heart trusts in him, and I am helped. My heart leaps for joy and I will give thanks to him in song.

2 Corinthians 5:20 (NIV) We are therefore Christ's ambassadors, as though God were making his appeal through us. We implore you on Christ's behalf: Be reconciled to God.

Proverbs 3:6 (NKJV) In all your ways acknowledge Him, And He shall direct your paths.

Psalm 37:23 (NLT) The Lord directs the steps of the godly. He delights in every detail of their lives.

Isaiah 45:3 (NLT) And I will give you treasures hidden in the darkness — secret riches. I will do this so you may know that I am the Lord, the God of Israel, the one who calls you by name.

Chapter Seven:

Matthew 7:8 (NLT) For everyone who asks, receives. Everyone who seeks, finds. And to everyone who knocks, the door will be opened.

Ephesians 6:10 (NLT) A final word: Be strong in the Lord and in His mighty power.

Psalm 114:8 (NLT) He turned the rock into a pool of water; yes, a spring of water flowed from solid rock.

Micah 6:8 (NLT) No, O people, the Lord has told you what is good, and this is what he requires of you: to do what is right, to love mercy, and to walk humbly with your God.

Proverbs 21:31 (NLT) The horse is prepared for the day of battle, but the victory belongs to the Lord.

Isaiah 60:22 (NLT) The smallest family will become a thousand people, and the tiniest group will become a mighty nation. At the right time, I, the Lord, will make it happen.

2 Timothy 3:16-17 (NKJV) All Scripture is given by inspiration of God, and is profitable for doctrine, for reproof, for correction, for instruction in righteousness, that the man of God may be complete, thoroughly equipped for every good work.

Colossians 2:7 (NLT) Let your roots grow down into him, and let your lives be built on him. Then your faith will grow strong in the truth you were taught, and you will overflow with thankfulness.

Job 13:15 (NKJV) Though He slay me, yet will I trust Him.

Isaiah 40:31 (NLT) But those who trust in the Lord will find new strength. They will soar high on wings like eagles. They will run and not grow weary. They will walk and not faint.

Hebrews 11:1 (NKJV) Now faith is the substance of things hoped for, the evidence of things not seen.

Hebrews 11:1 (NLT) Faith is the confidence that what we hope for will actually happen; it gives us assurance about things we cannot see.

Luke 17:5-6 (NLT) The apostles said to the Lord, "Show us how to increase our faith." The Lord answered, "If you had faith even as small as a mustard seed, you could say to this mulberry tree, 'May you be uprooted and thrown into the sea,' and it would obey you!"

Romans 12:12 (NIV) Be joyful in hope, patient in affliction, faithful in prayer.

James 2:26 (NKJV) For as the body without the spirit is dead, so faith without works is dead also.

Luke 8:11-15 (NLT) This is the meaning of the parable: The seed is God's word. The seeds that fell on the footpath represent those who hear the message, only to have the devil come and take it away from their hearts and prevent them from believing and being saved. The seeds on the rocky soil represent those who hear the message and receive it with joy. But since they don't have deep roots, they believe for a while, then they fall away when they face temptation. The seeds that fell among the thorns represent those who hear the message, but all too quickly the message is crowded out by the cares and riches and pleasures of this life. And so they never grow into maturity. And the seeds that fell on the good soil represent honest, good-hearted people who hear God's word, cling to it, and patiently produce a huge harvest.

Mark 4:26-27 (NLT) Jesus also said, "The Kingdom of God is like a farmer who scatters seed on the ground. Night and day, while he's asleep or awake, the seed sprouts and grows, but he does not understand how it happens.

Isaiah 7:9 (NLT) Unless your faith is firm, I cannot make you stand firm.

Luke 13:18-19 (NLT) Then Jesus said, "What is the Kingdom of God like? How can I illustrate it? It is like a tiny mustard seed that a man planted in a garden; it grows and becomes a tree, and the birds make nests in its branches."

Chapter Eight:

Matthew 5:14-16 (NLT) You are the light of the world—like a city on a hilltop that cannot be hidden. No one lights a lamp and then puts it under a basket. Instead, a lamp is placed on a stand, where it gives light to everyone in the house. In the same way, let your good deeds shine out for all to see, so that everyone will praise your heavenly Father.

Genesis 1:1-3 (NLT) In the beginning God created the heavens and the earth. The earth was formless and empty, and darkness covered the deep waters. And the Spirit of God was hovering over the surface of the waters. Then God said, "Let there be light," and there was light.

1 Peter 2:9 (NLT) But you are not like that, for you are a chosen people. You are royal priests, a holy nation, God's very own possession. As a result, you can show others the goodness of God, for he called you out of the darkness into his wonderful light.

Matthew 5:16 (NLT) In the same way, let your good deeds shine out for all to see, so that everyone will praise your heavenly Father.

Isaiah 6:8 (NLT) Then I heard the Lord asking, "Whom should I send as a messenger to this people? Who will go for us?" I said, "Here I am. Send me."

Numbers 14:15-16 (NLT) Now if you slaughter all these people with a single blow, the nations that have heard of your fame will say, "The Lord was not able to bring them into the land he swore to give them, so he killed them in the wilderness."

Romans 10:17 (NKJV) So then faith comes by hearing, and hearing by the word of God.

Ecclesiastes 4:12 (NLT) A person standing alone can be attacked and defeated, but two can stand back-to-back and conquer. Three are even better, for a triple-braided cord is not easily broken.

Matthew 18:20 (NLT) For where two or three gather together as my followers, I am there among them.

Matthew 6:14-15 (NKJV) For if you forgive men their trespasses, your heavenly Father will also forgive you. But if you do not forgive men their trespasses, neither will your Father forgive your trespasses.

Ephesians 4:30-32 (NLT) And do not grieve the Holy Spirit of God, with whom you were sealed for the day of redemption. Get rid of all bitterness, rage and anger, brawling and slander, along with every form of malice. Be kind and compassionate to one another, forgiving each other, just as in Christ God forgave you.

Romans 6:16 (NLT) Don't you know that when you offer yourselves to someone as obedient slaves, you are slaves of the one you obey—whether you are slaves to sin, which leads to death, or to obedience, which leads to righteousness?

Romans 6:16 (NLT) Don't you know that when you offer yourselves to someone as obedient slaves, you are slaves of the one you obey—whether you are slaves to sin, which leads to death, or to obedience, which leads to righteousness?

2 Corinthians 10:3-5 (NLT) For though we walk in the flesh, we do not war according to the flesh. For the weapons of our warfare are not carnal but mighty in God for pulling down strongholds, casting down arguments and every high thing that exalts itself against the knowledge of God, bringing every thought into captivity to the obedience of Christ.

Habakkuk 2:2 (NKJV) Write the vision, and make it plain on tablets, That he may run who reads it.

Isaiah 65:22 (NIV) No longer will they build houses and others live in them, or plant and others eat. For as the days of a tree, so will be the days of my people; my chosen ones will long enjoy the works of their hands.

ACKNOWLEDGMENTS

I am sure there are some who sit down to write a book and, within a few months, it comes into being. I am not in that company. I knew nearly two decades ago that I would one day write this book, but I never dreamed it would be the product of such an extensive learning journey. Every job seeker who has participated in small groups with me has been a contributor to this effort as we sought the heart of God together. They are, unfortunately, too many to name. Perhaps those whose stories are told here will smile as they recognize themselves and remember again how they encountered God in their seasons out of the workplace. I am grateful that I had the privilege of sharing in all their journeys and witnessing their faith and courage as they sought to conduct their job searches "God's way."

Many faithful friends and co-laborers have supported me through various seasons of this job seeker ministry. Two are no longer in this earthly realm, but I want to remember them for the love and generous support they poured into my life. Thank you, Charlotte Lemons, and thank you, Dad. Others—Pat Milner, Gail Fowler, and Raye Varney—gave of themselves in the very beginning to help me capture ideas and get them down on paper as we first began to understand what God had in mind for His children in the workplace. Your efforts gave me the starting point for this book. Cathy Vollmer and Andrea Andreasen joined me later in the journey to offer ideas, encouragement and support. Across the years I've also been blessed with the prayer covering of wonderful intercessors who have faithfully covered me, my family and the small group ministry. I could not have done this without you, Jennifer Alexander, Cheryl Hasson, Susan Yeyeodu and especially you, Mom. Fran Browning, you especially have steadfastly been with me for nearly this entire journey. I cannot imagine what my life would have been like without all your ideas, encouragement and support.

Stan, my husband, you are in a category all your own. You have not only read, reread and edited this manuscript countless times, but you have also put this message to the test as you walked through seasons of unemployment and applied it in your life. You've ministered in small groups with me, taken those frantic job seeker phone calls, and washed countless dishes after all the job seeker meetings in our home. I cannot express how much your faith in this message and your support has meant to me.

I also owe an enormous debt of gratitude to Tim Krauss for catching the spirit of this book and introducing it to Crown Financial Ministries. Thank you, Jan Strydom, for embracing this message and becoming its strong advocate; Megan Pacheco for the enormous energy you invested in keeping everything on track and moving forward; and, Jim Henry and Jim Armstrong for all the care, wisdom, guidance, and expertise you invested so that this message could be released in the workplace. I have been so richly blessed by all of you!

Finally, I would like to bow before Jesus Christ, my Lord, and give thanks for the privilege of working on this assignment. I pray that this book will bring Him glory and will bless the body of Christ in a manner fully pleasing to Him.